THE ALLOCATION
OF TIME AND GOODS
OVER THE LIFE CYCLE

NATIONAL BUREAU OF ECONOMIC RESEARCH

Human Behavior and Social Institutions

THE ALLOCATION
OF TIME AND GOODS
OVER THE LIFE CYCLE

GILBERT R. GHEZ
and
GARY S. BECKER

University of Chicago and
National Bureau of Economic Research

NATIONAL BUREAU OF ECONOMIC RESEARCH
New York   1975
Distributed by COLUMBIA UNIVERSITY PRESS
New York and London

Relation of the Directors to the Work and Publications of the National Bureau of Economic Research

1. The object of the National Bureau of Economic Research is to ascertain and to present to the public important economic facts and their interpretation in a scientific and impartial manner. The Board of Directors is charged with the responsibility of ensuring that the work of the National Bureau is carried on in strict conformity with this object.

2. The President of the National Bureau shall submit to the Board of Directors, or to its Executive Committee, for their formal adoption all specific proposals for research to be instituted.

3. No research report shall be published by the National Bureau until the President has sent each member of the Board a notice that a manuscript is recommended for publication and that in the President's opinion it is suitable for publication in accordance with the principles of the National Bureau. Such notification will include an abstract or summary of the manuscript's content and a response form for use by those Directors who desire a copy of the manuscript for review. Each manuscript shall contain a summary drawing attention to the nature and treatment of the problem studied, the character of the data and their utilization in the report, and the main conclusions reached.

4. For each manuscript so submitted, a special committee of the Directors (including Directors Emeriti) shall be appointed by majority agreement of the President and Vice Presidents (or by the Executive Committee in case of inability to decide on the part of the President and Vice Presidents), consisting of three Directors selected as nearly as may be one from each general division of the Board. The names of the special manuscript committee shall be stated to each Director when notice of the proposed publication is submitted to him. It shall be the duty of each member of the special manuscript committee to read the manuscript. If each member of the manuscript committee signifies his approval within thirty days of the transmittal of the manuscript, the report may be published. If at the end of that period any member of the manuscript committee withholds his approval, the President shall then notify each member of the Board, requesting approval or disapproval of publication, and thirty days additional shall be granted for this purpose. The manuscript shall then not be published unless at least a majority of the entire Board who shall have voted on the proposal within the time fixed for the receipt of votes shall have approved.

5. No manuscript may be published, though approved by each member of the special manuscript committee, until forty-five days have elapsed from the transmittal of the report in manuscript form. The interval is allowed for the receipt of any memorandum of dissent or reservation, together with a brief statement of his reasons, that any member may wish to express; and such memorandum of dissent or reservation shall be published with the manuscript if he so desires. Publication does not, however, imply that each member of the Board has read the manuscript, or that either members of the Board in general or the special committee have passed on its validity in every detail.

6. Publications of the National Bureau issued for informational purposes concerning the work of the Bureau and its staff, or issued to inform the public of activities of Bureau staff, and volumes issued as a result of various conferences involving the National Bureau shall contain a specific disclaimer noting that such publication has not passed through the normal review procedures required in this resolution. The Executive Committee of the Board is charged with review of all such publications from time to time to ensure that they do not take on the character of formal research reports of the National Bureau, requiring formal Board approval.

7. Unless otherwise determined by the Board or exempted by the terms of paragraph 6, a copy of this resolution shall be printed in each National Bureau publication.

(Resolution adopted October 25, 1926, and revised through September 30, 1974)

Contents

Tables

Figures

Introduction

GILBERT R. GHEZ and
GARY S. BECKER

This book, which deals with the allocation of resources by families over the lifetime of their members, is part of a rapidly growing literature on the economics of the household that views family formation, dissolution, acquisition of skills, and the use of resources as amenable to economic analysis. In this volume, we concentrate on the allocation of time and the consumption of goods by family members over their life cycle. We present a powerful theory with a variety of implications, and offer evidence that the theory is consistent with observed lifetime behavior.

Economists have in the past paid little attention to life cycle behavior. While the importance of future events in current decision making has been recognized at least as long ago as in Irving Fisher's study of consumption behavior, typically economists have not sought to give a systematic explanation of observed variations in behavior with age; even in the voluminous work on the consumption function only a tiny fraction has been devoted to variations in consumption with age. The direction pioneered by Irving Fisher and more recently by Milton Friedman has not been followed in the analysis of labor supply: students of labor supply have been slow to incorporate the effect of future variables on current participation. Although some writers have distinguished between the transitory component and the permanent component of wage variables in labor supply analysis, the underlying form is usually not rigorously developed.

One major implication of this neglect has been that in analyzing cross-sectional data, economists have for the most part not clearly separated those effects that are age-related from those that are not. Similarly, little sorting has been attempted in time series analysis between those effects which are related to age and those which are related to calendar time.

The importance of improving our understanding of life cycle behavior is underscored by the increasing selectivity of government policy. During the 1960s there was an enormous surge in public expenditures on education, with young persons being the prime beneficiaries, at least initially. Other groups in the population are voicing their concerns. Efforts are being made to reduce the cost of child care to women, so that fewer women would need to withdraw from the labor force during their twenties and thirties. The aged are becoming increasingly vocal, perhaps in response to the shifting age distribution of the population.

It is our contention that the paucity of thinking and empirical work on life cycle behavior is related to some gaps in existing theories. In this volume we therefore propose a basic model for the analysis of life cycle behavior, and offer a series of empirical tests of its implications.

One premise of our analysis is that families take account of expected future events when making decisions. A second premise is that time is a scarce resource. Therefore, families are forced to allocate their time in an efficient way, just as they are forced to make efficient choices about the uses of their incomes. Families make decisions about their participation in the work force concurrently with consumption and savings decisions. In the literature on the consumption function it is generally assumed that labor force participation and income from work are fixed by factors outside the household's control, although research in labor supply has yielded repeated evidence to the contrary. The interrelation between these decisions provides considerable insight into the life cycle patterns of both the labor supply and consumption.

A third premise is that families engage in activities that require both time and goods for their realization. This is the sense of the so-called characteristics or production function approach to consumption decisions. The basic notion is that little useful output can be obtained from goods unless time at home is available and similarly for time without goods. It emphasizes that households are producers and consumers wherever they go, not just producers at work and consumers at home. In studies done in the last few years, this approach has provided a powerful framework for analyzing many kinds of household behavior, in particular, the demand for recreational goods, the demand for health, the effects of differences in income and education on labor supply and expenditures on goods, etc.[1]

From these premises we derive a series of novel implications. We show, for instance, that the number of hours supplied to the market is expected to be positively related to the price of time over the life cycle. This explains why people work hardest when their market productivity is greatest and why they retire at old age when their productivity is low. Previous analyses have yielded ambiguous predictions because of the difficulties experienced in separating substitution and income effects.

We also show that consumption is expected to change in a definite way over the life cycle as the price of time changes. We show that under suitable parameter restrictions, consumption would be positively related to the price of time over the lifetime: it would rise more rapidly the more rapidly the wage rate was rising. There is much accumulated evidence showing that persons having more schooling have more rapidly rising earnings capacities.[2] Our theory predicts that they would also have more rapidly rising consumption levels. We predict that consumption would rise in response to seasonal and cyclical upswings. On the other hand, the relation between consumption and age, at least in the framework of perfect capital markets and no uncertainty, essentially cannot be explained by applying the standard analysis of consumption planning. Indeed, in the latter, the smoothing of the income stream is stressed in an extreme form, whereby consumption would be constant over the life cycle, barring interest rate effects, time preference effects and the effects of changes in family size.

We also consider the acquisition of skills by family members over their lifetime. We show how optimal life cycle investment in human capital is determined and explain why investment tends eventually to

1. See, for instance, Reuben Gronau, *The Value of Time in Passenger Transportation: The Demand for Air Travel* (New York: NBER, Occasional Paper 109, 1970); Robert Michael, *The Effect of Education on Efficiency in Consumption* (NBER, Occasional Paper 116, 1972); Michael Grossman, *The Demand for Health: A Theoretical and Empirical Investigation* (NBER, Occasional Paper 119, 1972); Arleen Leibowitz, "Woman's Allocation of Time to Market and Nonmarket Activity" (Ph.D. diss., Columbia University, 1972); Robert Willis, "A New Approach to the Economic Theory of Fertility Behavior," *Journal of Political Economy,* vol. 81 (March/April 1973), pp. 14–64.

2. See in particular Jacob Mincer, *Schooling, Experience, and Earnings* (New York: NBER, 1974).

fall with age. Many of the interesting issues in human capital investment theory and the relation between such investments and labor
supply and consumption are sketched out but not fully developed
here.

Other aspects of family planning are introduced in a more casual
way. For instance, little attention is paid to the optimal timing of
children, and no attention is paid to the timing of marriage and sepa-
ration, although these too bear on consumption behavior. We believe,
however, that the basic structure laid out in this book will provide a
convenient framework for research on these issues.

Much of this book is devoted to testing the theory with empirical
evidence. For this purpose the BLS Survey of Consumer Expenditures for 1960–61 and the 1/1,000 Census sample [3] of the U.S. population for 1960 are systematically exploited. We devise a methodology
for using the empirical data to isolate life cycle effects, and show that
these data are generally consistent with the implications of the
theory. In particular, we find there are sizable positive responses of
both consumption and labor supply to variations in the price of time
over the life cycle, when we hold some other determinants fixed. We
also find evidence of substitution between goods and husband's
time, and between husband's time and wife's time. These estimates
are combined at the end of this book to predict the effect of changes
in the price of time unrelated to the life cycle; in particular, the effect
on secular changes in labor supply and consumption of the secular
growth in real wage rates over the last half century. The predicted
values of consumption and hours of work are in general the same as
the observed values of the variables over the last fifty years. We also
find that the estimates are consistent with the observed procyclical
responses of consumption and labor force participation. In summary,
we believe that the basic model of time in home production has wide
applicability and strong explanatory power. Its strength lies in its
ability to interpret vastly different bodies of data.

Our discussion is organized into four chapters. In the first one
we present the theoretical model. In the second, we discuss the
empirical methodology and report on estimates of the life cycle consumption function of different groups in the population. In the third,

3. See Chapter 3, Note 36, below.

we present estimates of the life cycle labor supply function for different groups. In the fourth, we integrate the estimates in the second and third chapters, and suggest some further applications.

Most of the material in this volume was completed several years ago. Since that time several other studies of life cycle allocation of time and goods have been developed. We believe that our theoretical analysis goes somewhat further than these other studies do, and that our empirical analysis of life cycle behavior is the most extensive and most clearly related to the theoretical analysis.

Since this work is a mixture of jointly credited and separately credited material, it may be useful to describe more precisely the relative contributions of each of the authors. Becker is mainly responsible for developing the basic model and for the empirical work on hours of work of men reported in Chapter 3. Ghez is responsible for developing the derived demand equations given in the text, for much of the empirical procedure used throughout this volume, and for his results on consumption patterns in Chapter 2. He is also mainly responsible for the discussion of the human capital model and its interaction with consumption decisions.

Acknowledgments

This study was conducted mainly at the National Bureau of Economic Research and funded by grants from the Carnegie Corporation and the Carnegie Commission on Higher Education, for whose financial assistance we are very grateful.

This book is the result of a substantial research effort over the last several years. Since its publication has been delayed, we have benefited from concurrent and subsequent research carried out by others. However, the original thrust and flavor of the book remain.

We are grateful to Jacob Mincer for his constructive comments at every stage of this project; to Robert Michael and Michael Grossman, who offered continued discussion of virtually every aspect of this book and whose research efforts overlapped ours in part; to the members of the National Bureau's Staff Reading Committee, James Heckman, F. Thomas Juster, and Warren Sanderson, for many useful comments; to members of the Workshop in Applications of Economics at the University of Chicago, in particular H. Gregg Lewis, and to members of the Labor Workshop at Columbia University.

We also thank Haim Ofek and Barry Geller for excellent research assistance; Charlotte Boschan, Susan Crayne, and Sidney Jacobs for their valuable help in solving computer problems; Ester Moskowitz for editing the manuscript; and H. Irving Forman for drawing the charts.

Finally, Ghez owes a special thanks to his wife, Susanne, for her continued encouragement and for bearing part of the costs of a long process of creation.

THE ALLOCATION
OF TIME AND GOODS
OVER THE LIFE CYCLE

1

A Theory of the Allocation of Time and Goods Over the Life Cycle

1.1 ASSUMPTIONS AND EQUILIBRIUM CONDITIONS

The three main building blocks of our analysis are: (i) the now traditional Fisherian theory of consumption planning over time; (ii) the
recent approach to the allocation of time that treats it on equal foot-
ing with the allocation of goods; (iii) the household production function approach that considers time and goods not as objects of choice
in utility functions but as inputs into the production of household
outputs that are these objects. This marrying of the old and the new
permits us to obtain novel results while preserving much of the
Fisherian format.

In order to simplify the presentation and bring out the main
points we make several assumptions that are relaxed later on. Each

NOTE: We consider ourselves equally important contributors to this chapter.
Becker's primary contribution is his unpublished paper, "The Allocation of Time and
Goods Over Time" (June 1967), and Ghez's is a series of papers starting in 1966 and
culminating in "A Theory of Life Cycle Consumption" (Ph.D. diss., Columbia University, 1970). Ghez is solely responsible for Chapter 2 and Becker for Chapter 3. We
are equally responsible for Chapter 4.

decision unit is assumed to be a single person rather than the more common multiperson families. Each unit is assumed to know with perfect certainty its life expectancy, utility function, production functions, flows of goods and time, and all other relevant magnitudes. Calendar time is divided into T periods of equal length, called years, and a single output is assumed to be produced in each period with a household production function that is the same in each period. The arguments in the production function are the service flows of goods and time. We assume that all goods are nondurable; this assumption is relaxed in Chapter 2. Time can be allocated to only two sectors: the market sector, where command over goods is received in return, or the nonmarket sector, where it is used directly to produce household outputs. In particular, we rule out any allocation of time (or goods) to the production of human capital.

Symbolically, these assumptions are expressed in a series of relations for each decision unit between the input of goods and time and the output of what we shall henceforth call commodities:

$$C_t = F(X_t, L_t), \qquad t = 1, 2, \ldots, T. \quad (1.1)$$

where X_t is the aggregate input of the services of goods in the tth period, L_t is the input of the individual's own time, and C_t is his output of commodities.[1] The C_t in principle can be measured and observed, but they are not marketable; instead they enter directly into the utility function:

$$U = U(C_1, C_2, \ldots, C_T). \quad (1.2)$$

This function depends on the stream of present and future commodity flows.

By substituting the relations given by equation (1.1) into equation (1.2), we get the "derived" utility function of goods and time:

$$U = U[F(X_1, L_1), F(X_2, L_2), \ldots, F(X_T, L_T)]$$

$$= V(X_1, X_2, \ldots, X_T; L_1, L_2, \ldots, L_T). \quad (1.3)$$

A full justification of our decision to restrict the presentation to the seemingly more complicated two-stage formulation given by equations (1.1) and (1.2), rather than the simple utility function of equation

---

1. C_t is to be thought of as a quantity index over all nonmarket outputs. For a more disaggregated analysis, see Ghez, "Life Cycle Consumption," App. A.

(1.3) is presented elsewhere.[2] Here we only point out that the two-stage formulation emphasizes the special relation between goods and time in the same period compared to the relation between goods and time from randomly selected periods. Put more technically, the two-stage formulation implies that goods and time of the same period can be separated in the derived utility function; that is, the ratio of their marginal utilities does not depend on the goods and time of other periods.[3]

Let N_t denote the time an individual spends at market activities, usually called "work," during his tth year of age, and θ the length of each time period. Since we have assumed that time can be used only at work or in producing consumption,[4] we have the following T time constraints:[5]

$$L_t + N_t = \theta, \qquad t = 1, 2, \ldots, T. \quad (1.4)$$

where L_t, $N_t \geq 0$. By its very nature time cannot be transferred directly from one period to another, but we show later that it can be transferred indirectly.

If goods can be transferred between periods, consumption of goods at age t, unlike consumption of time, will not be limited by the

---

2. See Robert T. Michael and Gary S. Becker, "On the New Theory of Consumer Demand," *Journal of Swedish Economics,* vol. 75 (1973), pp. 378–396; and Kelvin Lancaster, *Consumer Demand—A New Approach* (New York: Columbia University Press, 1971).

3. Since

$$\frac{\partial U}{\partial X_t} = \frac{\partial U}{\partial C_t} \frac{\partial F}{\partial X_t}$$

and

$$\frac{\partial U}{\partial L_t} = \frac{\partial U}{\partial C_t} \frac{\partial F}{\partial L_t},$$

then

$$\frac{\partial U}{\partial X_t} \Big/ \frac{\partial U}{\partial L_t} = \frac{\partial F}{\partial X_t} \Big/ \frac{\partial F}{\partial L_t} = H(X_t, L_t).$$

4. In particular, we rule out the use of time in savings or in asset management. The analysis can easily be extended to cover these cases.

5. C_t, X_t, L_t, and N_t have the dimensions of total quantities produced and consumed during period t of length θ. Alternatively, and with no change in substance, the analysis could proceed with all variables defined as within-period rates (say $c_t = C_t/\theta$, $x_t = X_t/\theta$, $l_t = L_t/\theta$); accordingly, the sum of the proportions of time spent on each activity would equal unity in each period.

flow of resources at t but by the discounted value of the whole lifetime flow. Let R_t be the value at the beginning of period zero of one dollar received at age t:

$$R_t = 1/(1 + r_0)(1 + r_1) \ldots (1 + r_{t-1}), \qquad (1.5)$$

where r_t is the rate of interest in period t. Barring bequests, the budget constraint for goods may be written as

$$\sum_{t=1}^{T} R_t p_t X_t = \sum_{t=1}^{T} R_t w_t N_t + A_0, \qquad (1.6)$$

where p_t is the price of a unit of services of market goods at age t, w_t is the wage rate at t, and A_0 is the discounted value of property income, i.e., initial assets. Substituting the T time constraints of equation (1.4) into equation (1.6), we obtain: [6]

$$\sum_{t=1}^{T} R_t(p_t X_t + w_t L_t) = \sum_{t=1}^{T} R_t w_t \theta + A_0. \qquad (1.7)$$

If both wage rates and interest rates at each year of age were given and were independent of an individual's behavior and if all his time were spent at work, the right-hand side of equation (1.7) would be the discounted value of money income, which we call "full wealth." [7] It is the sum of "full human wealth" and nonhuman wealth. The left side of equation (1.7) shows how full wealth is spent: in part directly on

---

6. Equation (1.7) may be rewritten in terms of real prices alone. The left-hand side is

$$\sum_{t} R_t(p_t X_t + w_t L_t) = \sum_{t} R_t p_t \left(X_t + \frac{w_t}{p_t} L_t \right) = p_0 \sum_{t} R_t^*(X_t + w_t^* L_t),$$

where $w_t^* = (w_t/p_t)$ and

$$R_t^* = \frac{(1 + \bar{p}_0)(1 + \bar{p}_1) \ldots (1 + \bar{p}_{t-1})}{(1 + r_0)(1 + r_1) \ldots (1 + r_{t-1})}; \; \bar{p}_t = \frac{p_{t+1} - p_t}{p_t}.$$

The right-hand side of equation (1.7) is

$$\sum_{t} R_t w_t \theta + A_0 = \sum_{t} R_t p_t \frac{w_t}{p_t} \theta + A_0 = p_0 \left(\sum_{t} R_t^* w_t^* \theta + A_0^* \right),$$

where $A_0^* = (A_0/p_0)$. Hence we have the full-wealth constraint with prices expressed in terms of goods in period 0:

$$\sum_{t} R_t^*(X_t + w_t^* L_t) = \sum_{t} R_t^* w_t^* \theta + A_0^*.$$

7. By analogy with the "full-income" concept developed by Becker in "A Theory of the Allocation of Time," *Economic Journal* (September 1965), pp. 493–517.

goods and in part indirectly by using time for consumption rather than at work.

We assume a person maximizes his utility subject to the constraints given by the production functions and full wealth. If the utility and production functions are twice differentiable, necessary conditions for an interior maximum include: [8]

$$\frac{\partial U}{\partial C_t} = \lambda R_t \pi_t; \qquad\qquad t = 1, 2, \ldots, T. \quad (1.8)$$

$$\pi_t = \frac{w_t}{\partial F_t / \partial L_t} = \frac{p_t}{\partial F_t / \partial X_t}; \quad t = 1, 2, \ldots, T. \quad (1.9)$$

where $\partial U / \partial C_t$ is the marginal utility (at the beginning of the initial period) of commodity consumption at age t, λ is the marginal utility of wealth, π_t is the marginal cost of producing commodities at age t, and $\partial F_t / \partial L_t$ and $\partial F_t / \partial X_t$ are the marginal products of consumption time and market goods respectively at age t.

Conditions (1.8) state that the marginal utility of commodity consumption at any age should be proportional to the discounted value of the marginal cost of producing commodities at that age. Put differently, the marginal rate of substitution between commodity consumption at any two ages should equal the ratio of their discounted marginal costs. If C_t is decreased by a small amount, π_t dollars of resources are released in the form of X_t or L_t, or a combination of the two. The goods released may be lent at the market rate r_t.[9] Although time is not transferable between periods, its yield is: a reduction in L_t means a rise in work in t and hence a rise in income, which also may be lent at rate r_t. The increment in income next period of $\pi_t(1 + r_t)$ buys $\pi_t(1 + r_t)/\pi_{t+1}$ units of C_{t+1}. In equilibrium, the willingness to substitute commodity consumption at time $t + 1$ for commodity consumption at t should equal the cost of increasing commodity consumption at $t + 1$ in lieu of commodity consumption at t.

Conditions (1.9) are the familiar cost minimization conditions. At each age, the increment in output from an additional dollar "spent" on time should equal the increment in output from an additional

---

8. The corner solution obtained when no time is spent at work is discussed briefly in section 6.

9. If money prices of goods are changing over time, the net return from lending one unit of goods in period t is equal to the real rate of interest, $r_t - \bar{p}_t$.

dollar spent on goods. If factor proportions were fixed, conditions (1.9) would be discarded and marginal cost would equal the increase in total cost when both factors are increased in fixed proportions.

In the remainder of this study, we assume that the production functions are homogeneous of the first degree: a 1 per cent increase in goods combined with a 1 per cent increase in time in period t increases commodity output by 1 per cent. This assumption appears to be rather innocuous, especially at the level of abstraction we deal with. Taken together with the assumption that wage rates are independent of hours of work, the assumption of constant returns to scale ensures that household production will be subject to constant unit costs. Hence, the marginal cost at age t, denoted by π_t, is independent of the level of commodity output at t.

1.2   MARKET PRODUCTIVITY EFFECTS OVER THE LIFE CYCLE

In this and the next several sections we analyze some implications of the model just set out. Our interest in this study is centered on the life cycle: we seek to explain the allocation of goods and time over the life cycle.[10] Our primary focus is on the demand for market goods and time, because these data are used to test the model. The pattern of consumption of commodities is described only enough to make the pattern of derived demand for goods and time understandable.

The basic method of analysis is to decompose the changes in the demand for goods and consumption time into substitution between goods and time in production, and substitution between commodities in consumption. Equation (1.9) can be written as

$$\frac{\partial F/\partial L_t}{\partial F/\partial X_t} = \frac{w_t}{p_t}. \tag{1.10}$$

This states that, in equilibrium, the marginal rate of substitution in production is equal to the ratio of factor prices, which is the opportunity cost of time expressed in terms of goods, or, for short, the real wage rate. Taking equations (1.10) and (1.11) together, we can ex-

---

10. Although the comparative statistics of the model are not discussed, the fundamental principles of demand analysis apply here. In particular, a fall in the marginal cost of C_t compensated for so as to hold real wealth constant increases the amount of C_t consumed.

press the demand for goods and consumption time at age t as functions of the real wage rate and household output at t

$$X_t = X(w_t/p_t, C_t); \tag{1.11}$$

$$L_t = L(w_t/p_t, C_t). \tag{1.12}$$

An increase in the real wage rate induces substitution away from the relatively more expensive factor of production. If the real wage rate rose over time and household output were held constant, the demand for goods would increase while the demand for consumption time would fall. Therefore, substitution of factors in production makes the demand for goods positively related and the demand for consumption time negatively related to the wage rate over the life cycle.

Even if output varied systematically with the real wage rate, the *ratio* of goods to time must rise with the real wage rate, for if the production function is homogeneous, the ratio of the marginal product of goods to the marginal product of time depends only on the quantity of goods relative to time. Consequently, the demand for goods relative to time would be independent of household output,[11] and would be positively related to the wage rate over time: it would rise as the real wage rate rose, and fall as the real wage rate fell.

The percentage change in the demand for goods relative to time due to a 1 per cent change in the real wage rate is given by the elasticity of substitution in production. Let σ_f denote this elasticity, and let $\tilde{x}_t = (x_{t+1} - x_t)/x_t$ for any variable x. Then the change in goods intensity at time t is described by [12]

$$\tilde{X}_t - \tilde{L}_t = \sigma_f(\tilde{w}_t - \tilde{p}_t),$$

$$\sigma_f \geqslant 0; \ t = 1, 2, \ldots, T - 1. \tag{1.13}$$

where $\tilde{w}_t - \tilde{p}_t$ is the percentage change in the real wage rate at time t. For any given change in the real wage rate, the change in the demand

---

11. Given homogeneity of the production function, a 1 per cent increase in output raises the demand for all inputs by the same proportion when factor prices are held constant. In particular, with a homogeneous production function of the first degree we have $X(w/p, C) = x(w/p)C$ and $L(w/p, C) = l(w/p)C$.

12. This equation holds as an approximation if σ_f is interpreted as the point elasticity of substitution evaluated at, say, the point w_t/p_t.

for goods relative to time is larger, the larger the elasticity of substitution in production.

Consider now the effects of substitution between commodities in consumption on the demand for goods and time. At constant factor prices, an increase in commodity output increases the demand for both goods and consumption time.[13] How does this output vary with age? Since perfect foresight and constant tastes have been assumed, there would be no unanticipated changes in real wealth with age. Therefore, variations in commodity consumption with age would not be due to wealth effects; they would be entirely due to time preference and to substitution effects generated by anticipated variations in prices with age.

The relevant prices for commodity consumption decisions are discounted commodity prices. Indeed, equilibrium conditions (1.8) state that the marginal utility of commodity consumption in period t should be proportional to the marginal cost of commodities in period t discounted to the initial period. Put differently, the marginal rate of substitution between commodity consumption in any periods t and $t+1$ should equal the ratio of their discounted prices:

$$\frac{\partial U/\partial C_t}{\partial U/\partial C_{t+1}} = \frac{R_t \pi_t}{R_{t+1} \pi_{t+1}}.$$

$$t = 1, 2, \ldots, T-1. \quad (1.14)$$

From these conditions, we get the demand function for commodity consumption at any age t,

$$C_t = C(R_1 \pi_1, R_2 \pi_2, \ldots, R_T \pi_T, t, U), \quad (1.15)$$

where U is the utility index.

It is intuitively plausible that in the absence of time preference, commodity consumption would be relatively high during periods when the discounted cost of producing commodities was relatively low. Preference for the present makes early consumption relatively more attractive, whereas preference for the future makes later consumption relatively more attractive.

These implications can be derived more formally by imposing certain restrictions on the utility function. We assume that the

---

13. Inferior factors are ruled out by the assumption that the production function is homogeneous.

marginal rate of substitution between commodity consumption at time t and $t+1$ depends only on the commodities consumed at those two dates; it is independent of consumption at all other times. Second, we assume that all indifference curves between consecutively dated commodities are symmetric.[14] These two assumptions combined imply that the marginal rate of substitution between t and $t+1$ can be written as

$$\frac{\partial U/\partial C_t}{\partial U/\partial C_{t+1}} = \beta_{t,t+1} \frac{g(C_t)}{g(C_{t+1})},$$

$$t = 1, 2, \ldots, T-1. \quad (1.16)$$

with $g' < 0$.

Neutral time preference is said to exist if the marginal utilities of C_t and C_{t+1} are the same when $C_t = C_{t+1}$. There is preference for the present or for the future as the marginal utility of C_t is greater than or smaller than the marginal utility of C_{t+1} when $C_t = C_{t+1}$. In other words

$$\left.\left(\frac{\partial U/\partial C_t}{\partial U/\partial C_{t+1}}\right)\right|_{C_t=C_{t+1}} \begin{matrix} > 1 \\ = 1 \\ < 1 \end{matrix} \Bigg\} \text{ defines} \begin{cases} \text{preference for the present} \\ \text{neutral time preference} \\ \text{preference for the future} \end{cases}$$

In terms of equations (1.16), preference is for the present, for the future, or for neither as $\beta_{t,t+1}$ is greater than, smaller than, or equal to unity. By substituting equations (1.16) into the intertemporal equilibrium conditions (1.14), we obtain:

$$\beta_{t,t+1} \frac{g(C_t)}{g(C_{t+1})} = \frac{R_t \pi_t}{R_{t+1} \pi_{t+1}}.$$

$$t = 1, 2, \ldots, T-1. \quad (1.17)$$

---

14. The first assumption implies that the lifetime utility function is additively separable. For a proof, see William Gorman, "Conditions for Additive Separability," *Econometrica* (July–October 1968), pp. 605–609. The second assumption implies that the rate of time preference is independent of wealth. Together, these assumptions imply that the utility function may be written as

$$U = \sum_{t=1}^{T} \beta_t \, G(C_t),$$

where in equation (1.16)

$$g(G_t) \equiv \frac{\partial G}{\partial C_t}$$

$$\beta_{t,t+1} \equiv \beta_t / \beta_{t+1}.$$

It will be convenient to transform all prices into real prices. Let R_t^* denote the value in terms of goods in the initial period of one unit of goods received in t, and let π_t^* denote the marginal cost of commodities in period t in terms of goods in period t: $\pi_t^* = \pi_t/p_t$. Then the equilibrium conditions (1.17) can be written equivalently as

$$\beta_{t,t+1} \frac{g(C_t)}{g(C_{t+1})} = \frac{R_t^* \pi_t^*}{R_{t+1}^* \pi_{t+1}^*},$$

$$t = 1, 2, \ldots, T-1.$$

(1.18)

$$= (1 + r_t^*) \frac{\pi_t^*}{\pi_{t+1}^*},$$

$$t = 1, 2, \ldots, T-1.$$

where r_t^* is the real rate of interest in period t.

Assume for the moment that the real rate of interest is equal to zero, and that time preference is neutral ($\beta_{t,t+1} = 1$ for all t). Then conditions (1.18) become

$$\frac{g(C_t)}{g(C_{t+1})} = \frac{\pi_t^*}{\pi_{t+1}^*}. \quad t = 1, 2, \ldots, T-1. \quad (1.19)$$

Since $g' < 0$, commodity consumption would rise or fall over time as the real marginal cost of producing commodities falls or rises. Put differently, the household shifts its consumption toward periods when the real cost of consumption is relatively low, for in so doing it achieves the maximum possible lifetime utility consistent with its resources.[15]

Real marginal costs depend only on the real wage rate (the opportunity cost of time used in household activities), because we have assumed constant returns to scale and constant household technology. Since time is important in home production, marginal costs would be relatively high when the wage rate was relatively high: they would rise together, peak at the same age, and fall together. It follows from equations (1.19) that commodity consumption would be falling

---

15. In other words, if $G(C_t)$, in note 14, is identified as the household's per period level of utility (= real income), then it will be low when the cost of consumption is relatively high.

FIGURE 1.1
CONSUMPTION OF COMMODITIES OVER THE LIFE CYCLE

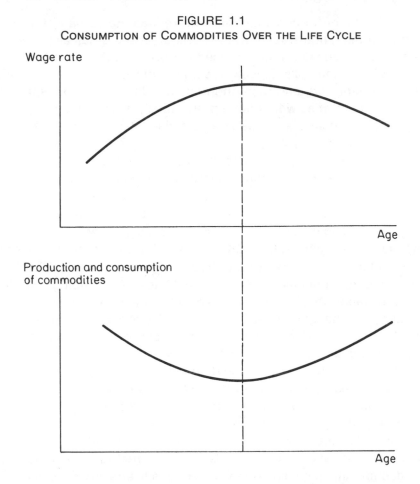

when the wage rate was rising and rising when the wage rate was falling;[16] in Figure 1.1 these patterns are portrayed over the life cycle.

Variations in the wage rate with age set in motion two effects: substitution between goods and time of the same period and substitution between commodities of different periods. While the wage rate is rising, a household substitutes goods for time and present commodities for future ones. Therefore, substitution in production

___

16. The conclusion that commodity consumption is inversely related to the wage rate (at a given level of real income) does not depend on the assumption of constant costs (or constant returns to scale). If costs were a rising function of output, the same rise in costs over time would simply make the decline in home consumption somewhat smaller than if costs were independent of output.

and substitution in consumption both reduce the demand for consumption time: hours spent in the nonmarket sector fall as the wage rate rises because less time is used per unit of output and because the level of output falls. Since wage rates typically rise rapidly initially with age, taper off, and then often fall at older ages, hours spent in household activities would fall rapidly initially, taper off, and reach a trough at the peak wage rate age, and rise later on when the wage rate fell (see Figure 1.2).

Since we assume that time can be allocated only to market or consumption activities, hours spent in the market, i.e., hours at "work," would be positively related to the wage rate over the life cycle. They would rise as long as the wage rate rose and fall when the wage rate fell. In the standard analysis of the supply of labor, a rise in the wage rate generates a substitution effect in favor of working time and an income effect away from it. The income effect is often supposed to dominate and cause a "backward-bending" supply curve of labor. In our analysis there is no income or wealth effect because all changes in wealth are perfectly foreseen. Hence a rise in wage rates with age generates only substitution effects, and the supply curve of labor would be positively sloped.[17]

The life cycle pattern of the demand for market goods is not as clearly defined as that for home time. As the wage rate rises with age, the demand for goods increases relative to home time. If output were stationary, the absolute demand for goods would also rise. However, as the wage rate rises, commodity consumption falls, and this reduces the demand for both goods and time, that is, substitutions in production and in consumption have opposite effects on the demand for goods: to predict the direction of change in the demand for goods as the wage rate varies, it is essential to know the relative strengths of these two substitution effects. If substitution in production is easier than in consumption, a household will increase its consumption of goods as wage rates rise and decrease it when wage rates fall. The opposite will be true if substitution in consumption is easier. These two types of paths of goods consumption are displayed in the bottom panel of Figure 1.2.

More formally, it can be shown that with neutral time preference

---

17. This conclusion is not a negation of the observation that a parametric shift in the wage profile generates both income and substitution effects.

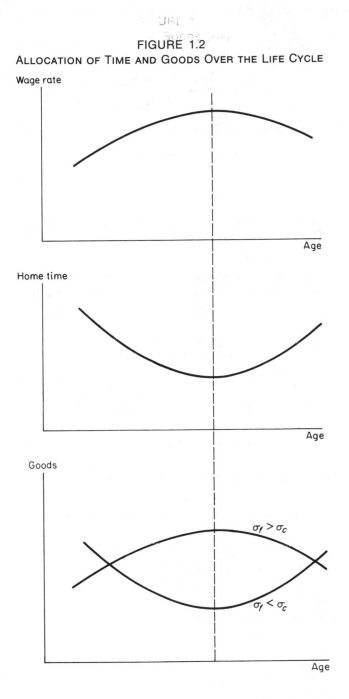

FIGURE 1.2
ALLOCATION OF TIME AND GOODS OVER THE LIFE CYCLE

and zero interest rates, the change in the demand for consumption time is related to the change in the wage rate as follows: [18]

$$\tilde{L}_t = -[\sigma_f(1 - s_t) + \sigma_c s_t](\bar{w}_t - \bar{p}_t).$$

$$t = 1, 2, \ldots, T - 1. \quad (1.20)$$

Similarly, the change in the demand for market goods is

$$\tilde{X}_t = (\sigma_f - \sigma_c)s_t(\bar{w}_t - \bar{p}_t),$$

$$t = 1, 2, \ldots, T - 1. \quad (1.21)$$

where

$\bar{w}_t - \bar{p}_t =$ percentage change in the real wage rate during period t;

$\sigma_f =$ elasticity of substitution between goods and time in production, $\sigma_f \geq 0$;

$\sigma_c =$ elasticity of substitution in consumption, $\sigma_c \geq 0$;

$s_t =$ proportion of household production costs accounted for by time during period t; $s_t = w_t L_t / (p_t X_t + w_t L_t)$.

The elasticity of substitution in consumption, σ_c, measures the percentage change in commodity demand due to a 1 per cent change in its price, whereas the proportion of forgone earnings in total costs, s, measures the percentage change in the marginal cost of commodities due to a 1 per cent change in the wage rate. Therefore, $-\sigma_c s$ measures the percentage change in commodity demand due to a 1 per cent change in the wage rate. Since the production function is assumed to be homogeneous of the first degree, substitution in consumption is the same for goods and time as it is for commodities. This explains why $-\sigma_c s$ enters both equations (1.20) and (1.21).

Substitution in production, however, has different effects on goods and time. On goods the effect is measured by $\sigma_f s$, whereas on consumption time it is measured by $-\sigma_f(1 - s)$. A 1 per cent increase in the wage rate raises goods intensity, or the demand for goods *relative* to time, by σ_f per cent. A 1 per cent increase in goods intensity at constant output raises the absolute demand for goods by s per cent and reduces the absolute demand for time by $(1 - s)$ per cent.

Since σ_f, σ_c, and s are nonnegative numbers (s has a maximum

---

18. Equations (1.20)–(1.23), (1.25), and (1.26) are approximations. Abstracts of proofs are given in the appendix. Complete proofs are contained in Ghez, "Life Cycle Consumption."

value of unity), the implication of equation (1.20) is that a change in the demand for consumption time is negatively related to a change in the wage rate. The change in demand is a weighted average of the elasticity of substitution in consumption and in production. The direction of the change in the demand for market goods, on the other hand, is not clear a priori and depends on the difference between these elasticities. Changes in the demand for goods will be positively or negatively related to changes in the wage rate as the elasticity of substitution in production is greater than or less than the elasticity of substitution in consumption.[19]

1.3 EFFECTS OF THE INTEREST RATE AND OF TIME PREFERENCE

We have been assuming neutral time preference and a zero interest rate. A positive interest rate reduces the value of discounted future commodity prices relative to present ones, and thus induces a substitution toward future commodities, consumption time, and goods relative to present ones. By contrast with variations in the price of time, however, positive interest rates do not affect the optimal combination of factors. The ratio of goods to time is independent of the rate of interest,[20] and depends only on the concurrent real wage rate [see equation (1.10)].

Given a zero rate of interest and neutral time preference, the consumption of commodities and time will fall as the wage rate rises, reach a trough at the peak wage age, and then rise. Therefore, a positive interest rate will push the trough to an earlier age than the peak wage age. Put differently, the peak in hours of work will come earlier than the peak wage rate. If goods rise with the wage rate ($\sigma_f > \sigma_c$), the peak in goods consumption will be pushed to a later age than the peak wage rate age.[21] If the rate of interest is sufficiently high, the

---

19. Since σ_f can depend on the real wage rate and σ_c on the level of commodity consumption, the difference ($\sigma_f - \sigma_c$) could be positive for some values and negative for other values of w_t^* and C_t along a given life cycle path.

20. This implication is no longer true in a model incorporating durable consumer goods. On this point, see Chapter 2.

21. By the same reasoning, if goods fell when the wage rate rose ($\sigma_f < \sigma_c$), the trough in goods consumption would occur earlier than the peak wage rate age.

trough in commodity and time consumption will come at the initial age and the peak in goods at the terminal age; hence, all three will rise continuously over the life cycle.[22]

Time preference for the future has the same kind of effect as a positive interest rate: it encourages future consumption relative to present consumption, but does not affect the optimal combination of factors. The troughs in the consumption of commodities and time will fall earlier and the peak in goods later than the peak wage rate. Preference for the present has precisely the opposite effects.

Equations (1.20) and (1.21) are easily modified to accommodate the effects of the interest rate and of time preference. Changes in consumption time are now described by

$$\tilde{L}_t = -[\sigma_f(1-s) + \sigma_c s](\tilde{w}_t - \tilde{p}_t) + \sigma_c(r_t - \tilde{p}_t - \rho_t);$$

$$t = 1, 2, \ldots, T-1. \quad (1.22)$$

and changes in goods, by

$$\tilde{X}_t = (\sigma_f - \sigma_c)s(\tilde{w}_t - \tilde{p}_t) + \sigma_c(r_t - \tilde{p}_t - \rho_t);$$

$$t = 1, 2, \ldots, T-1. \quad (1.23)$$

where $r_t - \tilde{p}_t$ is the real rate of interest at time t, and ρ is an index of time preference [23] that is positive, negative, or zero depending on whether preference is for the present, the future, or neither. Only the difference between the rates of interest and time preference enters these equations.[24] They affect time and goods in exactly the same way because we have assumed that the production functions are homogeneous.

In equations (1.22) and (1.23) the changes in time and goods are decomposed into more fundamental determinants: changes in wage rates and in interest rates net of time preference. The Fisherian model of lifetime planning as developed by Modigliani and associates

---

22. Note that if the rate of interest net of time preference were positive, multiple extremes could occur in the consumption paths for commodities, time, and goods (even if the path of the wage rate had only a single peak) if $\tilde{w}$ did not decline monotonically, if the share of time, s, were variable, or if the rate of interest were variable. However, the last trough in time would precede, and the first peak in goods (assuming $\sigma_f > \sigma_c$) would occur after, the peak wage rate.

23. ρ_t and $\beta_{t,t+1}$ are related by: $\beta_{t,t+1} = 1 + \rho_t$.

24. This is borne out by the intertemporal equilibrium conditions (1.17).

neglects the first determinant and concentrates exclusively on the second.[25]

1.4   NONMARKET PRODUCTIVITY EFFECTS

In this section we examine the effect of variations in nonmarket productivity over time on the life cycle demand for goods and time. We need not at this point detail the sources of change in nonmarket efficiency; in the next section changes in both market and nonmarket efficiency are related to changes in the stock of human capital.

Changes in nonmarket efficiency are reflected in shifts in the productivity of goods and time in the household production functions. Formally, the production function at age t can be written as:

$$C_t = F(X_t, L_t; t). \qquad (1.24)$$

To begin with, notice that the utility-maximizing conditions set out in equation (1.8) and (1.9) or in equations (1.10) and (1.17) still hold, but that the marginal products of goods and time now depend not only on input proportions but also on age itself (t). Changes in age result in either an increase or decrease in the output producible with given inputs. For simplicity, in the following discussion we talk only about improvements with age.

Technological improvement with age raises the marginal product of goods, consumption time, or both, in future periods relative to present ones, for given levels of these inputs. It thus lowers the marginal cost of commodities in future periods compared to present ones, and induces substitution toward future commodities.

The effect on the derived demand for goods and time depends on the magnitude of the output response relative to the saving in inputs generated by the technological improvement. The output response is measured by the elasticity of substitution in consumption: a 1 per cent fall in marginal costs generates a σ_c per cent rise in the consumption of commodities. On the other hand, there would be a 1 per

25. See Franco Modigliani and Richard Brumberg, "Utility Analysis and the Consumption Function: An Interpretation of Cross-Section Data," in K. Kurihara, ed., *Post-Keynesian Economics* (New Brunswick: Rutgers University Press, 1954), pp. 383–436. Also Franco Modigliani and Albert Ando, "The 'Permanent Income' and the 'Life Cycle' Hypothesis of Saving Behavior: Comparison and Tests," in Irving Friend and Robert Jones, eds., *Proceedings of Conference on Consumption and Saving*, vol. 2 (Philadelphia: University of Pennsylvania Press, 1960), pp. 49–174.

cent reduction in the inputs needed to produce a given output. Hence, consumption of goods and time would rise along with technology if the elasticity of substitution in consumption were greater than unity, and would fall if the elasticity of substitution in consumption were smaller than unity.

The changes in consumption time and goods described by equations (1.22) and (1.23) can be expanded to include changes in non-market efficiency with age,

$$\tilde{L}_t = -[\sigma_f(1 - s) + \sigma_c s](\tilde{w}_t - \tilde{p}_t) + (\sigma_c - 1)\hat{F}_t + \sigma_c(r_t - \tilde{p}_t - \rho_t);$$

$$t = 1, 2, \ldots, T - 1. \quad (1.25)$$

$$\tilde{X}_t = (\sigma_f - \sigma_c)s(\tilde{w}_t - \tilde{p}_t) + (\sigma_c - 1)\hat{F}_t + \sigma_c(r_t - \tilde{p}_t - \rho_t);$$

$$t = 1, 2, \ldots, T - 1. \quad (1.26)$$

where $\hat{F}_t$ denotes the rate of change in nonmarket efficiency at time t.[26]

1.5   THE PRODUCTION OF HUMAN CAPITAL

We have been explaining the allocation of time and goods over a lifetime by life cycle variations in wage rates, nonmarket efficiency, interest rates, and preferences. The thrust of the substantial research during the last fifteen years on investment in human capital, however, has been precisely to show that variations in wage rates and even in nonmarket efficiency are not simply given: they are largely determined by investments in schooling, on-the-job training, health, preschooling, and other kinds of human capital.[27]

---

26. These equations assume Hicksian factor-neutral technological change. If the change is factor biased it is necessary to add $-\sigma_f(1 - s)B_t$ to equation (1.25) and $\sigma_f s B_t$ to (1.26), where $B_t = \widehat{MPX}_t - \widehat{MPL}_t$, with $\widehat{MPX}_t$ and $\widehat{MPL}_t$ measuring the percentage changes in the marginal products of goods and time at time t. Then $\hat{F}_t$ is a weighted average of these changes: $\hat{F}_t = (1 - s)\widehat{MPX}_t + s\widehat{MPL}_t$.

27. For an outstanding discussion of the effects of schooling and post-school investments, see Jacob Mincer, *Schooling, Experience, and Earnings* (New York: NBER, 1974). For interesting discussions of the effect of human capital on nonmarket efficiency, see Robert T. Michael, *The Effect of Education on Efficiency in Consumption*, NBER Occasional Paper 116 (New York: NBER, 1972) and Michael Grossman, *The Demand for Health: A Theoretical and Empirical Investigation*, NBER Occasional Paper 119 (New York: NBER, 1972).

The essence of the approach is to define a stock of human capital owned by each person; he can produce more, but since the capital is embodied in his own person and since even voluntary slavery is considered illegal, he cannot sell or buy any capital. Let H_t denote the stock of human capital he holds at the beginning of time t. The wage rate at t is assumed to be proportional to H_t

$$w_t = e_t H_t. \qquad t = 1, 2, \ldots, T. \quad (1.27)$$

Expressing this relationship in real prices, i.e., in terms of units of consumer goods, we have

$$w_t^* = e_t^* H_t, \qquad t = 1, 2, \ldots, T. \quad (1.28)$$

where $e_t^* = e_t/p_t$. The factor of proportionality e_t^* measures the service yield per unit of human capital for each hour spent at work at time t. The service yield can vary over time because of changes in the economy at large.

Human capital is produced by using own time and a bundle of market goods and services, which we call educational goods. Let h_t denote the amount of human capital produced at time t, and N_t' and X_t' the time and educational goods used in the production of h_t. The production function that relates these inputs and outputs is

$$h_t = h(N_t', X_t'). \qquad t = 1, 2, \ldots, T. \quad (1.29)$$

We are assuming for the present that H_t, the stock of human capital at t, does not affect the productivity of N_t' and X_t'. If human capital never depreciated, the change in its stock at any point would simply equal the amount produced. More generally, if δ_t denotes the rate of depreciation on this stock at age t, we have [28]

$$H_{t+1} = H_t(1 - \delta_t) + h_t.$$

$$t = 1, 2, \ldots, T - 1. \quad (1.30)$$

Gross investment at time t (h_t) equals net investment ($H_{t+1} - H_t$) plus depreciation ($\delta_t H_t$).

The amount of human capital held at any age can be expressed in terms of the undepreciated component of the initial inherited

---

28. Since the stock of human capital is durable, $\delta_t < 1$ for all t; and since nature by itself does not create human capital, $\delta_t \geq 0$ for all t.

stock [29] and the amounts previously produced:

$$H_t = H_1 D_{1,t} + \sum_{v=1}^{t-1} h_v D_{v+1,t},$$

$$t = 1, 2, \ldots, T. \quad (1.31)$$

where $D_{v,t}$ is the fraction of human capital held at age v and remaining at age t, i.e.,

$$D_{v,t} = (1 - \delta_v)(1 - \delta_{v+1}) \ldots (1 - \delta_{t-1}).$$

$$v = 1, 2, \ldots, t-1. \quad (1.32)$$

Equation (1.31) clearly shows that human capital held at any age depends on the past resources devoted to its production. Indeed, this may be confirmed by substituting the production function (1.29) into equation (1.31):

$$H_t = H_1 D_{1,t} + \sum_{v=1}^{t-1} h(N_v', X_v') D_{v+1,t}$$

$$= H(N_1', N_2', \ldots, N_{t-1}'; X_1', X_2', \ldots, X_{t-1}'; t; H_1).$$

$$t = 1, 2, \ldots, T. \quad (1.33)$$

We start with the seemingly more complicated two-stage formulation given by equations (1.29) and (1.31) rather than with the direct formulation given by equation (1.33) [30] because in the former the emphasis is on the special relationship that exists between investment time and educational goods used at the same time as compared to use of these inputs at different times. [31]

---

29. Since the initial age is arbitrary in our analysis, the initial stock depends on past accumulation. It also depends on the individual's native ability and on his environment.

30. In fact, once the two-stage formulation is dropped, the concept of a stock of human capital can also be dropped and replaced by a generalized wage rate function

$$w_t^* = w^*(N_1', N_2', \ldots, N_{t-1}'; X_1', X_2', \ldots, X_{t-1}'; t). \qquad t = 1, 2, \ldots, T.$$

31. Put more technically, the two-stage formulation implies that

$$\partial H_t / \partial N_v' = \psi_{N'}(N_v', X_v', t, v);$$

$$\partial H_t / \partial X_v' = \psi_{X'}(N_v', X_v', t, v). \qquad t = 1, 2, \ldots, T;$$

$$v = 1, 2, \ldots, t-1.$$

Any time used in the production of human capital must be diverted from other possible uses, namely, from working time and consumption time; hence, the time constraints become

$$L_t + N_t + N_t' = \theta. \quad t = 1, 2, \ldots, T. \quad (1.34)$$

Similarly, expenditures on educational goods compete with expenditures on consumption goods. If p_t' is the price of educational goods at time t, the budget constraint (1.6) is modified to

$$\sum_{t=1}^{T} R_t(p_t X_t + p_t' X_t') = \sum_{t=1}^{T} R_t w_t N_t + A_0. \quad (1.35)$$

If the time constraints (1.34) are substituted into the budget constraint (1.35), we obtain [32]

$$\sum_{t=1}^{T} R_t(p_t X_t + w_t L_t) + \sum_{t=1}^{T} R_t(p_t' X_t' + w_t N_t') = \sum_{t=1}^{T} R_t w_t \theta + A_0. \quad (1.36)$$

For the moment the production functions (1.1) are assumed to be unaffected by the accumulation of human capital.

---

32. The right-hand side of equation (1.36) measures the amount of wealth attainable if all time is spent at work, but no longer measures "full wealth," for it excludes the production of human capital. An increase in the production of human capital at time t would raise all future wage rates, and would therefore increase both the right-hand side of equation (1.36) and the cost of all household production beyond time t.

Full wealth can, however, still be meaningfully defined. Let $V(L_1, L_2, \ldots, L_T)$ denote the maximum value of consumable wealth when consumption time in each period is held at fixed levels $L_1, L_2, \ldots, L_T$. That is,

$$V(L_1, L_2, \ldots, L_T) = \max \left(\sum_t R_t w_t N_t - \sum_t R_t p_t' X_t' + A_0 \right),$$

given $L_1, L_2, \ldots, L_T$; hence

$$\sum_t R_t p_t X_t = V(L_1, L_2, \ldots, L_T).$$

Full wealth, W, is defined as the value of $V(L_1, L_2, \ldots, L_T)$ when no time is spent in consumption: $W = V(0, 0, \ldots, 0)$. If Ψ denotes the wealth forgone by using time to produce commodities, we have the full-wealth constraint:

$$\sum_t R_t p_t X_t + \Psi(L_1, L_2, \ldots, L_T) = W.$$

This is a development of the general definition of full income given in Becker, "Theory of Allocation." We recognize that the concept of full wealth does not add any new information to the analysis when prices are not parametric.

If utility is maximized subject to the budget constraint given by equation (1.35), the production functions for human capital [equation (1.29)] and household commodities [equation (1.24)], and the human capital constraints given by equation (1.31), the necessary conditions for an interior maximum include the following:

$$\frac{\partial U}{\partial C_t} = \lambda R_t \pi_t. \qquad t = 1, 2, \ldots, T. \qquad (1.37)$$

$$\pi_t = \frac{w_t}{\partial F/\partial L_t} = \frac{p_t}{\partial F/\partial X_t} \cdot \quad t = 1, 2, \ldots, T. \qquad (1.38)$$

$$\mu_t = \frac{w_t}{\partial h/\partial N_t'} = \frac{p_t'}{\partial h/\partial X_t'} \cdot \qquad (1.39)$$

$$R_t \mu_t = \sum_{v=t+1}^{T} R_v e_v D_{t,\,v-1} N_v. \qquad (1.40)$$

The equilibrium conditions (1.37) and (1.38) are identical to equations (1.8) and (1.9), the equilibrium conditions derived when the production of human capital was excluded. (For a modification, see page 28.) Consequently, our analysis of the paths of commodities, consumption time, and goods in the previous sections is not affected by allowing human capital to be endogenous. Put differently, the question of whether these paths are rising or falling as the wage rate is rising or falling is completely independent of the reasons for changes in the wage rate. This fundamental proposition is at the heart of all the empirical work reported in this volume.

The new equilibrium conditions due to the accumulation of human capital are given by equations (1.39) and (1.40). According to equation (1.39), at each point in time the increment in human capital (h) from an additional dollar of expenditure on time equals the increment from an additional dollar spent on educational goods. These define the marginal cost of producing human capital, which is μ_t at time t.

The left-hand side of equation (1.40), namely $R_t \mu_t$, yields the discounted value of the marginal cost of producing human capital, while the right-hand side yields the discounted value of returns from an additional unit of such capital. The term $e_v D_{t,\,v-1} = e_v(\partial H_v/\partial h_t)$ is the increase in the wage rate, and $e_v D_{t,\,v-1} N_v$ is the increase in earnings at time v attributable to an additional unit of human capital produced at time t. The discounted value of the increase in earnings measures the benefit from additional production at time t.[33] Of course, in equilibrium, the marginal cost of production should equal the marginal benefit.

It will be convenient for further analysis to express costs and returns from investment at time t in terms of consumer goods at time t, rather than in terms of dollars in the initial period. Dividing both sides of equation (1.40) by $R_t p_t$, we obtain:

$$\mu_t^* = B_t^w, \tag{1.41}$$

where $\mu_t^* = \mu_t/p_t$; and

$$B_t^w = \sum_{v=t+1}^{T} R_{v,t}^* e_v^* D_{t,v-1} N_v; \tag{1.42}$$

with $e_v^* = e_v/p_v$; and

$$R_{v,t}^* = \frac{R_v^*}{R_t^*} = 1/(1 + r_t^*)(1 + r_{t+1}^*) \dots (1 + r_{v-1}^*).$$

Correspondingly, equation (1.39) becomes

$$\mu_t^* = \frac{w_t^*}{\partial h/\partial N_t'} = \frac{p_t'^*}{\partial h/\partial X_t'}, \tag{1.43}$$

where $p_t'^* = p_t'/p_t$. From this condition and the production function for human capital, we get the marginal cost function for human capital

$$\mu_t^* = \mu^*(w_t^*, p_t'^*, h_t). \tag{1.44}$$

Henceforth it is assumed that the price of educational goods relative to consumption goods remains unchanged over time; therefore, $p_t'^* = p_t'/p_t$ is a constant.

Whether real wage rates rise or fall over time depends on whether the stock of human capital and the index e_t^* are rising or falling.

---

33. Note that actual hours worked are used in the evaluation of benefits no matter how they vary by age or level of human capital. In rate-of-return calculations, if the difference in the amounts invested is small, it will not matter whether hours of work of the unskilled or of the skilled group are used, since the effect on real income of any differences in hours worked induced by the different amounts invested is of second-order smallness. On the other hand, for large differences in amounts invested, using hours of work of the unskilled group will understate returns, while using hours of work of the skilled group will overstate returns.

Indeed, from equation (1.28),

$$\tilde{w}_t^* = \tilde{e}_t^* + \tilde{H}_t. \quad t = 1, 2, \ldots, T-1. \quad (1.45)$$

The stock of human capital rises or falls depending on whether the output of human capital is larger or smaller than depreciation. If human capital never depreciated ($\delta_t = 0$ for all t), then its stock could never decrease with age, and would increase so long as some human capital were being produced. Human capital is being produced in period t if and only if the equality (1.40) or (1.41) holds for period t.

The time path of the output of human capital is implicit in the set of equilibrium conditions. Suppose for the moment that human capital never depreciated (hence $D_{t,v} = 1$ for all v, t), that the index e_v^* was constant, and that the real rate of interest was always equal to zero. Then, if human capital is being produced at time t, the stock of human capital will be higher in $t+1$ than in t (since $\delta_t = 0$), and, therefore, the real wage rate will be higher in $t+1$ than in t (since $\tilde{e}_t^* = 0$). Hence the marginal cost function of producing human capital will be higher in $t+1$ than in t. This provides one incentive for producing human capital early in life rather than later.

How do benefits from producing human capital at time t compare with benefits at later ages? Since the depreciation rate, interest rates, and the growth in efficiency of a unit of human capital are all assumed to equal zero, marginal benefits cannot increase. The change in marginal benefits would equal $-eN_{t+1}$, i.e., the loss in the service yield provided by an additional output of human capital when this addition is produced in $t+1$ rather than in t. Therefore, as long as some time is spent at work, marginal benefits must fall with age.

Since marginal benefits fall and marginal costs rise with age, the optimal production of human capital necessarily falls with age. Hence our analysis predicts the well-known finding that the real wage rate rises with age at a decreasing absolute rate.[34]

Time spent in the production of human capital must fall with age both because output falls and because of the inducement to substitute away from time and in favor of educational goods as the price of time rises.[35] Since investment time falls as the wage rate rises, and since we showed earlier that consumption time also falls as the wage

---

34. See, for example, Mincer, *Schooling*.

35. The demand for educational goods would fall or rise over time depending on whether the effect of output expansion was greater or smaller than the effect of factor substitution.

rate rises (barring time preference effects), hours of work would rise as the wage rate rises. The effect of the decline in consumption time on working time is reinforced by the decline in investment time.

If human capital depreciates, the stock of human capital and hence the real wage rate will decline toward the end of life, when the incentive to invest becomes small. On the other hand, growth in the efficiency of a unit of human capital causes the wage rate to rise beyond the age where net investment ceased. Indeed, depreciation and efficiency have symmetrical and opposite effects on the wage rate: [36]

$$w_{t+1}^* - w_t^* = e_t^*(H_{t+1} - H_t) + H_t(e_{t+1}^* - e_t^*)$$

$$= e_t^*[h_t - (\delta_t - \tilde{e}_t^*)H_t].$$

$$t = 1, 2, \ldots, t - 1. \quad (1.46)$$

Once we drop the assumptions of zero depreciation and interest rates and constant efficiency, marginal benefits may rise for a while with age (they must ultimately decline of course). If they rose faster than marginal costs, the output of human capital would also rise with age for a while.[37]

---

36. In the equation, $-\tilde{e}_t^*$ might be defined as the rate of obsolescence on human capital at time t.

37. If equilibrium condition (1.40) holds for periods t and $t + 1$, by taking first differences we obtain $\mu_{t+1}^* - \mu_t^* = B_{t+1}^w - B_t^w$. But since

$$B_{t+1}^w - B_t^w = -e_{t+1}^* N_{t+1} + (r_t^* + \delta_t) B_t^w$$

and

$$\mu_{t+1}^* - \mu_t^* = \frac{\partial \mu^*}{\partial w_t^*} (w_{t+1}^* - w_t^*) + \frac{\partial \mu^*}{\partial h_t} (h_{t+1} - h_t),$$

then solving for $h_{t+1} - h_t$, we obtain

$$h_{t+1} - h_t = \frac{-\dfrac{\partial \mu^*}{\partial w_t^*} (w_{t+1}^* - w_t^*) - e_{t+1}^* N_{t+1} + (r_t^* + \delta_t) B_t^w}{\dfrac{\partial \mu^*}{\partial h_t}}.$$

Converting this expression into percentage changes, and using the relation $w_t^* = e_t^* H_t$, we have

$$\tilde{h}_t = \frac{-s_t' \dfrac{h_t}{H_t} - \dfrac{e_{t+1}^* N_{t+1}}{B_t^w} + s_t'(\delta_t - \tilde{e}_t^*) + r_t^* + \delta_t}{\dfrac{h_t}{\mu_t^*} \dfrac{\partial \mu^*}{\partial h_t}},$$

where

$$s_t' = \frac{w_t^*}{\mu_t^*} \frac{\partial \mu^*}{\partial w_t^*}.$$

If output of human capital falls monotonically with age, so will the time spent in its production.[38] Therefore, hours of work will rise as the wage rate rises because both consumption time and training time will fall.[39] If the difference between the rates of interest and time preference is zero, consumption time will reach a trough at the peak wage age, whereas the trough in training time will come later if human capital depreciates and its efficiency does not change with age. Hence, working time will peak later than the trough in consumption time, but will tend to decline eventually because the rise in consumption time will more than offset any fall in training time.

Marginal benefits at any age are positively related to the rate of output of human capital at that age, as shown by the curves B_t and B_t' in Figure 1.3.[40] Finite nonzero investment could occur only if marginal cost rose faster than marginal benefit as output of human capital rose.

If the production function for human capital given in equation (1.29) is homogeneous of the first degree, the marginal cost of producing human capital at any age will be independent of output as long as the value of time is given by the (assumed) fixed market wage rate at that age. If so much human capital is being produced that all of working time is drawn into its production, the value of time can no longer be measured by the market wage rate, since no more time will be available at that price. Additional time will have to be drawn from consumption, and the value of time in producing additional human capital will then be measured by the money equivalent of the marginal productivity of time in consumption. As more and more time is drawn out of consumption, this marginal productivity will rise, and so will the shadow price of time and the marginal cost of producing human

---

38. An exception might occur if wages fell eventually while gross output continued to be positive, because the substitution toward time induced by the declining wages could increase the time spent in training.

39. Measured working time often includes training time. For a further discussion, see Chapter 3.

40. A proof of this statement can be developed along the following lines: An increase in output of human capital at age t, with future levels of output held constant, raises the future stock of human capital. The resulting higher future wages induce substitution away from training and consumption times. Future hours of work, and thus marginal benefits at age t, rise as output of human capital rises at age t.

This point is further developed in Gilbert R. Ghez, "A Note on the Earnings Function When Human Capital Is Biased Toward Earnings" (unpublished, February 1973).

FIGURE 1.3
PRODUCTION OF HUMAN CAPITAL AT A GIVEN YEAR OF AGE

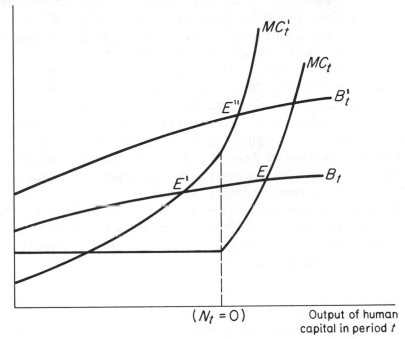

Marginal cost, marginal
benefit of human capital
production in period t

$(N_t = 0)$

Output of human
capital in period t

capital. The marginal cost curve, MC in Figure 1.3, is infinitely elastic until all working time is exhausted ($N_t = 0$) and then rises as consumption time is reduced.

Since benefits are a nondecreasing function of output, an equilibrium with positive investment is attained only if no time is spent at work. With marginal benefit schedule B_t and marginal cost schedule MC_t, equilibrium output is E in Figure 1.3, where no time is spent at work. The value of time is then measured by the consumption shadow price. That is, the following equality holds:

$$w_t^s = B_t^w \frac{\partial h}{\partial N_t'}, \tag{1.47}$$

where w_t^s is the value of the marginal hour spent in consumption.

If the production function for human capital exhibited diminishing returns to scale, say because new knowledge could only be absorbed at a decreasing rate, the marginal cost function would rise throughout (see MC'_t in Figure 1.3) and the equilibrium hours of work could readily be positive (see point E'). Of course, with sufficiently large benefits, the equilibrium could be at a "corner" even if marginal costs were rising throughout (point E'').

Specifying diminishing returns to scale is an ad hoc way of ensuring that positive investment will occur even when some time is spent at work. A more appealing alternative is to suppose that the production of human capital is homogeneous of the first degree not only in goods and training time, but also in working time. This, after all, is the rationale for on-the-job training: productivity is enhanced by combining work and training. Human capital will be produced with increasing cost even if working time is positive because working time and training time (and goods) can be increased in the same proportion only if consumption time is reduced. The reduction in consumption time, not diminishing returns, causes marginal costs to rise.[41]

If, for whatever reason, the equilibrium hours of work are zero for several ages — "corner equilibriums" — the change over time in benefits during these ages will be

$$\Delta B^w_t = -e^*_{t+1} N_{t+1} + (r^*_t + \delta_t) B^w_t = (r^*_t + \delta_t) B^w_t, \tag{1.48}$$

---

41. In this formulation, the production function of human capital would be $h_t = h(N_t, N'_t, X'_t)$, rather than (1.29), and equilibrium conditions (1.38) and (1.39) would be replaced by

$$\pi_t = \frac{w^s_t}{\partial F/\partial L_t} = \frac{p_t}{\partial F/\partial X_t};$$

$$\mu_t = \frac{w^s_t}{\partial h/\partial N'_t} = \frac{p'_t}{\partial h/\partial X'_t};$$

where w^s_t is the shadow wage rate;

$$w^s_t = eH_t + \sum_{v=t+1}^{n} R_{v,t} e_v D_{t,v-1} N_v \frac{\partial h_t}{\partial N_t}.$$

An alternative formulation, which would also generate increasing costs, is to suppose that the depreciation rate on human capital is negatively related to its rate of utilization, say hours of work. For a general discussion of the relationship between depreciation and utilization, see Gilbert R. Ghez, "Life Cycle Demand for Durable Consumer Goods" (unpublished, February 1968); and Robert T. Michael and Edward P. Lazear, "On the Shadow Price of Children" (unpublished, December 1971).

since hours of work, N_{t+1}, are assumed to equal zero in this interval. Marginal benefits from investment and with them the equilibrium shadow wage rate will *rise* during this interval.[42] The potential market wage rate, eH, will also be rising during this interval, and must eventually overtake the shadow wage rate; that is, the marginal benefit and cost curves must eventually intersect at a point where $N_t > 0$. The value of the individual's time would then be measured by his observed wage rate.

We have been assuming that investment in human capital at any age raises only market wage rates at later ages. Yet it presumably also raises the efficiency of later production of human capital and commodities and of asset management; that is, the stock of human capital enters the production functions given by equations (1.1) and (1.31) and influences the rate of return on nonhuman wealth, r, as follows:

$$C_t = F(X_t, L_t; H_t, t); \qquad (1.49)$$

$$h_t = h(N'_t, X'_t, H_t, t); \qquad (1.50)$$

and

$$r^*_t = r(H_t, t); \qquad (1.51)$$

with

$$\frac{\partial C_t}{\partial H_t} \geq 0; \; \frac{\partial h_t}{\partial H_t} \geq 0; \; \frac{\partial r}{\partial H_t} \geq 0.$$

The more general set of equilibrium conditions that replaces equations (1.43) is:

$$\mu^*_t = B^w_t + B^c_t + B^h_t + B^r_t; \qquad (1.52)$$

where

$$B^c_t = \sum_{v=t+1}^{T} R^*_{v,t} \pi^*_v C_v \left(\frac{1}{C_v} \frac{\partial F_v}{\partial H_v} \right) D_{t,v-1};$$

$$B^h_t = \sum_{v=t+1}^{S} R^*_{v,t} e^*_v H_v \frac{\partial N'_v}{\partial H_v} D_{t,v-1};$$

$S =$ number of periods during which human capital is produced $(S < T)$; and

---

42. Therefore, once again, the consumption of commodities and time would tend to fall during this interval, and the change in goods would depend on the relative importance of substitution in production and consumption.

$$B_t^r = \sum_{v=t+1}^{T} R_{v+1,t}^* A_v^* \frac{\partial r}{\partial H_v} D_{t,v-1};$$

with

$(1/C_v)(\partial F_v/\partial H_v)$ = percentage reduction in the total cost of producing a given amount of C_v.

$\partial N_v'/\partial H_v$ = the reduction in the amount of training time in period v required to achieve a given amount of h_v (the level of education goods held constant).

$\partial r_v/\partial H_v$ = the rise in the rate of return on nonhuman wealth.

We do not discuss here the full implications of this widening of the benefits flowing from investments in human capital since they are not incorporated in the empirical discussion. We simply note that these increases in efficiency are benefits of investing in human capital that not only add to the total benefit of such investment and thus increase the amount invested at any age, but also affect its time profile. For example, an increase in the efficiency of producing human capital would reduce and perhaps reverse the tendency for the marginal cost of producing human capital to rise over time as its stock increases. This in turn would reduce the decline over time in the output of human capital, and could even result in a rise for a time.[43]

Second, the nonmarket benefits to investment in human capital depend on the percentage reduction in the total cost of producing commodities and on the planned stream of expenditures on commodities. In the particular case where human capital is time augmenting in the home, with the result that human capital carries neutral efficiency effects between work and home activities, the nonmarket returns would be simply the discounted value of the increase in cost of home time due to a small increment in human capital produced today.[44] Consequently, benefits would be positively related to

---

43. In note 36 we show that a rise over time in market benefits could also cause a temporary rise in the output of human capital.

44. Suppose the household production function were $C_t = F(H_t L_t, X_t)$. Then

$$\pi_t = \frac{e H_t}{\dfrac{\partial F}{\partial H_t L_t} H_t} = \frac{e}{\dfrac{\partial F}{\partial H_t L_t}};$$

and

home time and negatively related to market time. If human capital carried neutral efficiency effects across all sectors, including its own production, marginal benefits would depend on total time and would therefore decrease monotonically with age.

Third, the benefits in the form of increased efficiency in portfolio management are weighted by the planned asset holdings; therefore, the larger one's planned portfolio the larger the benefits to current investment.[45]

Our model of capital accumulation over a lifetime is related to the models developed by others in the last decade.[46] We have extended these models, however, by integrating consumption and investment decisions; in particular, the size of stock of human capital is assumed to affect efficiency in consumption as well as in market production, and the optimal allocation of time between work and "leisure" is determined simultaneously with the optimal accumulation of human capital. Efficiency in consumption is an added incentive to investment in human capital. By incorporating the effect of efficiency into the model, we are better able to explain why, say, men and women invest in different ways.[47] One consequence of making hours of work endogenous is that since they should rise with age until about the peak wage age and then decline, B^w, the benefit in higher wages resulting from investment in human capital, would decline

$$\frac{\partial F}{\partial H_t} = \frac{\partial F}{\partial H_t L_t} \, L_t.$$

Therefore, B_i^c in equation (1.52) would become

$$B_i^c = \sum_{v=t+1}^{T} R_{v,t}^{\star} e^{\star} L_t D_{t,v-1}.$$

45. For a further development, see Uri Ben-Zion and Isaac Ehrlich, "A Model of Productive Saving" (unpublished, October 1972).

46. See, for example, Gary S. Becker, *Human Capital,* 2nd ed. (New York: NBER, forthcoming) and *Human Capital and the Personal Distribution of Income,* Woytinsky Lecture 1 (Ann Arbor: University of Michigan Press, 1967); Yoram Ben-Porath, "The Production of Human Capital and the Life Cycle of Earnings," *Journal of Political Economy* (August 1967); and Assaf Razin, "Investment in Human Capital and Economic Growth: A Theoretical Study" (Ph.D. diss., University of Chicago, 1969).

47. The reason is that women spend relatively more time in consumption than men do. If, for equal amounts of time spent at home, the marginal product of women's home time is at least as large as that of men, and if men earn more than women per unit of time, then the family's optimal allocation of resources is to have men working more hours than their wives. This point was first made by Haim Ofek in "The Allocation of Goods and Time in a Family Context" (Ph.D diss., Columbia University, 1971).

more slowly initially and more rapidly ultimately than in models in which constant hours of work are assumed.

1.6   MULTIPLE EARNERS

We now relax the assumption that the household is composed of only one person, and assume instead that it is composed of a husband and wife. The allocation of time of both members is determined simultaneously. The production function for commodities is still assumed to be homogeneous of the first degree, and can be written as

$$C_t = F_t(X_t, L_{1t}, L_{2t}),$$ (1.53)

where L_{1t} and L_{2t} denote the consumption time of husband and wife at age t of the household head.

If N_{1t} and N_{2t} are the time at work and w_{1t} and w_{2t} the wage rates of husband and wife at age t of the head, the budget constraint becomes

$$\sum_{t=1}^{T} R_t p_t X_t = \sum_{t=1}^{T} R_t(w_{1t}N_{1t} + w_{2t}N_{2t}) + A_0.$$ (1.54)

If all production of human capital is ignored for the present, the time constraints are

$$L_{1t} + N_{1t} = \theta;$$
$$L_{2t} + N_{2t} = \theta;$$ (1.55)

with $L_{it} \geq 0$, $N_{it} \geq 0$; $i = 1, 2$. If the constraint on goods given by equation (1.54) is combined with the time constraints of equations (1.55), we get the family full-wealth constraint:

$$\sum_{t=1}^{T} R_t(p_t X_t + w_{1t}L_{1t} + w_{2t}L_{2t}) = \sum_{t=1}^{T} R_t(w_{1t}\theta + w_{2t}\theta) + A_0.$$ (1.56)

To maximize the utility function given by (1.2), subject to the full-wealth constraint of equation (1.56), necessary conditions (for an interior solution) must include

$$\frac{\partial U}{\partial C_t} = \lambda R_t \pi_t;$$ (1.57)

$$\pi_t = \frac{p_t}{\partial F_t/\partial X_t} = \frac{w_{1t}}{\partial F_t/\partial L_{1t}} = \frac{w_{2t}}{\partial F_t/\partial L_{2t}}.$$ (1.58)

The marginal cost of commodities at age t of the head, π_t, depends now on the wage rate at that age of both members. The equilibrium conditions given by equations (1.57), which determine how commodity output is distributed over time, continue to hold.

If the difference between the rate of interest and time preference equals zero, the consumption of commodities will rise or fall with age as their marginal cost rises or falls. If the household production function is the same at all ages, consumption will rise or fall as the real wage rates of the husband and wife rise or fall. If both their wage rates rise, consumption will fall, whereas if the wage rate of one member rises while that of the other falls, the change in marginal cost and hence in consumption will depend on the relative magnitudes of the changes in wage rates and on the importance of each member's time in the production of commodities.

Changes in real wage rates induce substitution effects between factors of production as well. If the husband's real wage rate rises while the wife's remains stationary, the demand for husband's time will fall relative to the demands for goods and wife's time as long as goods and wife's time are substitutes for husband's time in the production of commodities.

Therefore, if the real wage rate of the husband rises while that of the wife remains constant, substitution in production and in consumption will both reduce the demand for his time. Her time will also fall only if the elasticity of substitution between the two time inputs is less than the elasticity of substitution in consumption; a similar conclusion holds for goods.

The changes in demand for goods and time given by equations (1.25) and (1.26) are replaced by the following: [48]

---

48. These equations assume factor-neutral technological change. If they were biased, one would add to equation (1.60) the terms

$$-(s_1\sigma_{11} + 1)B_1 - s_2\sigma_{12}B_2 - s_x\sigma_{1x}B_x;$$

to equation (1.61), the terms

$$-s_1\sigma_{21}B_1 - (s_2\sigma_{22} + 1)B_2 - s_x\sigma_{2x}B_x;$$

and to equation (1.62), the terms

$$-s_1\sigma_{x1}B_1 - s_2\sigma_{x2}B_2 - (s_x\sigma_{xx} + 1)B_x;$$

with $B_1 = \widehat{MPL_1} - \hat{F}$; $B_2 = \widehat{MPL_2} - \hat{F}$; $B_x = \widehat{MPX} - \hat{F}$; where $\widehat{MPL_1}$, $\widehat{MPL_2}$, and $\widehat{MPX}$ measure the percentage increases in the marginal products of L_1, L_2, and X, and $\hat{F}$ measures the percentage reduction in the marginal cost of commodities: $\hat{F} = s_1\widehat{MPL_1} + s_2\widehat{MPL_2} + s_x\widehat{MPX}$.

$$\tilde{L}_{1t} = s_1(\sigma_{11} - \sigma_c)(\tilde{w}_{1t} - \tilde{p}_t) + s_2(\sigma_{12} - \sigma_c)(\tilde{w}_{2t} - \tilde{p}_t)$$
$$+ (\sigma_c - 1)\hat{F}_t + \sigma_c(r_t - \tilde{p}_t - \rho_t); \quad (1.59)$$

$$\tilde{L}_{2t} = s_1(\sigma_{21} - \sigma_c)(\tilde{w}_{1t} - \tilde{p}_t) + s_2(\sigma_{22} - \sigma_c)(\tilde{w}_{2t} - \tilde{p}_t)$$
$$+ (\sigma_c - 1)\hat{F}_t + \sigma_c(r_t - \tilde{p}_t - \rho_t); \quad (1.60)$$

$$\tilde{X}_t = s_1(\sigma_{x1} - \sigma_c)(\tilde{w}_{1t} - \tilde{p}_t) + s_2(\sigma_{x2} - \sigma_c)(\tilde{w}_{2t} - \tilde{p}_t)$$
$$+ (\sigma_c - 1)\hat{F}_t + \sigma_c(r_t - \tilde{p}_t - \rho_t); \quad (1.61)$$

where

s_1 and s_2 = proportions of total costs of commodities accounted for by husband's and wife's time;

σ_{ij} = partial elasticity of substitution between factors i and j $(i, j = L_1, L_2, X)$, with $\sigma_{ii} < 0$ and $\sigma_{ij}(j \neq i) > $ or < 0 as i and j are substitutes or complements.[49]

Husbands and wives are not in the labor force at all ages. Both retire eventually as their market earnings are reduced due to failing health, reductions in their human capital, restrictions of social security legislation, etc. Wives often remain out of the labor force at younger ages as well, partly because their wage rates are low relative to their husband's, and partly because their household productivity is relatively high—primarily because of the presence of young children in the home.

1.7 FAMILY SIZE

We have been assuming that the number of persons in a family is exogenously given and is constant over time. Considerable research

---

49. There are certain restrictions on these partial elasticities of substitution. Let σ denote the matrix

$$\sigma = \begin{bmatrix} \sigma_{xx} & \sigma_{x1} & \sigma_{x2} \\ \sigma_{1x} & \sigma_{11} & \sigma_{12} \\ \sigma_{2x} & \sigma_{21} & \sigma_{22} \end{bmatrix}$$

σ is negative semidefinite. In particular, it is symmetric; all diagonal elements are negative (nonpositive); and $\sigma s = 0$, where s is the column vector (s_x, s_1, s_2) of factor shares and 0 is the zero vector.

is now in progress by economists on the formation, growth, and dissolution of families.[50] The core of these studies is the assumption that family size and composition are decision variables, basically no different than the usual ones considered by economists. We do not seek in this chapter to integrate these decisions fully into those dealing with the allocation of lifetime resources, although ultimately that must be done.

We assume that the marriage decision is made exogenously, i.e., independently of decisions about the lifetime allocation of resources. The parent's utility function is assumed to depend not only on the commodities previously defined, but also on commodities measuring child services: the number and "quality" of children of given years of age at each age of the household head. The raising of children requires time, especially wife's time,[51] and goods. Thus, time and goods must be allocated between child services and other commodities.

We note here those implications of this model that are most relevant to the empirical work reported in the next three chapters. If only the real wage rate of, say, the husband rises with age, other inputs will be substituted for his time in the production of all commodities, including child services; and present commodities, again including child services[52] will be substituted for future ones.

If husband's and wife's time are substitutes in the production of all commodities, the demand for her time relative to his will increase over time, and will increase absolutely if the total substitution effect in production is stronger than the total substitution effect in consumption. Thus, once we allow for changes in family size, the substitutions in production and consumption incorporated in equations (1.59), (1.60), and (1.61) must be interpreted as reflecting the combined effects of all commodities, including child services.

50. An early study is Gary S. Becker, "An Economic Analysis of Fertility," in *Demographic and Economic Change in Developed Countries,* Universities–National Bureau Conference 11 (Princeton, N.J.: Princeton University Press for NBER, 1960). For more recent studies, see for instance, T. W. Schultz, ed., "New Economic Approaches to Fertility," *Journal of Political Economy,* March–April 1973, Part II; and Schultz, ed., "Marriage, Human Capital, and Fertility," ibid., March–April 1974, Part II.

51. The importance of wife's time has been demonstrated in several empirical studies. See, for instance, Jacob Mincer, "Market Prices, Opportunity Costs, and Income Effects," in C. Christ et al., eds., *Measurement in Economics* (Stanford: Stanford University Press, 1963). See also the references listed in the preceding note.

52. Unless an increase in present child services greatly reduced the marginal utility of other commodities in the future.

1.8   SUMMARY

In this chapter a model of a family's consumption, work time, and investment in human capital was constructed under three basic assumptions: First, the primal objects of choice entering the utility function are nonmarket activities, called commodities, and these commodities are produced with market goods and own time. Second, the household can allocate its time between nonmarket and market activities, including the production of own human capital, at prices governed by its productivity in each of these sectors. Third, the household is endowed with perfect foresight; hence it predicts accurately its life-span and all its future income, wages, and interest rates. Under these assumptions, the following principal implications were drawn:

i. At a zero rate of interest and with neutral time preference, consumption time will be inversely related to the wage rate over the life cycle.

ii. Again at a zero rate of interest and with neutral time preference, the consumption of goods will be positively related to the wage rate over the life cycle if substitution between goods and time is easier than intertemporal substitution between nonmarket activities produced at different points in time.

iii. With a positive rate of interest (or preference for the present), nonmarket time will reach a trough before the peak-wage-rate age, and consumption of goods will reach a peak after the peak-wage-rate age (if $\sigma_f > \sigma_c$).

iv. Changes in nonmarket productivity over the life cycle can modify these patterns. In particular, if improvements in nonmarket efficiency are neutral between goods and home time, they will lessen the rise in the demand for goods and increase the incentive to contract home time during periods of rising wages, provided the intertemporal elasticity of substitution between commodities produced at different points in time is less than unity.

v. The incentive to engage in the production of human capital is shown to depend on an individual's planned future working time, since market returns from current investment are larger the larger his attachment to the labor force.

vi. Nonmarket returns to human capital increase future efficiency in the home. These returns will be positively related to home time if human capital is time-augmenting in the home.

vii. Barring nonmarket returns to human capital, the production of human capital will rise during the early years of life, when the incentive to produce is so large that the household specializes by spending no time at work. Eventually the rate of production falls, since, to the extent that human capital is not transferred to one's children, the benefit from additional production must fall to zero at the end of life.

viii. Time spent investing in human capital will also rise initially if the production of human capital rises, and will eventually fall along with the output of human capital, unless the substitution effect between time and goods in its production is larger than the effect of the reduced scale of investments.

ix. Hours of work will rise initially and reach a peak later than home time reaches its trough. If the rate of interest net of time preference is zero, home time will reach a trough at the peak-wage-rate age, while working time will reach a peak later, essentially because training time is declining in the neighborhood of the peak-wage-rate age (regardless of the degree of substitutability between time and goods in human capital production).

APPENDIX

1   WAGE RATE AND INTEREST RATE EFFECTS

Notation:

t = age of household head.

C_t = consumption of commodities at age t.

L_{1t}, L_{2t} = time spent in consumption by husband and wife at age t.

N_{1t}, N_{2t} = time spent at work by husband and wife at age t.

w_{1t}, w_{2t} = money wage rate of husband and wife at age t.

X_t = consumption of market goods at age t.

p_t = price index of market goods at age t.

r_t = rate of interest at age t.

R_t = value in period zero of \$1.00 received at age t, i.e., $R_t = 1/(1 + r_0)(1 + r_1) \ldots (1 + r_{t-1})$.

A_t = assets at age t after consumption decisions have been made at that age.

Each variable carries only one time subscript because all plans are assumed to be consistent and realized.[53]

We have the following four sets of relations:

i. A production function for commodities:

$$C_t = F(X_t,\, L_{1t},\, L_{2t}); \qquad t = 1, 2, \ldots, T. \quad \text{(A1.1)}$$

which is assumed to be twice differentiable and homogeneous of the first degree. For the present the production function is also assumed to be the same at all ages.

ii. A utility function which is assumed to be twice differentiable and the same at all years of age of the head:

$$U = U(C_1,\, C_2,\, \ldots,\, C_T), \qquad\qquad \text{(A1.2)}$$

where T is the lifetime horizon measured in years. Later on, the utility function is specialized to the following additive form:

$$U = \sum_{t=1}^{T} \beta_t G(C_t). \qquad\qquad \text{(A1.3)}$$

iii. A budget constraint:

$$\sum_{t=1}^{T} R_t p_t X_t = \sum_{t=1}^{T} R_t(w_{1t} N_{1t} + w_{2t} N_{2t}) + A_0. \qquad \text{(A1.4)}$$

iv. A set of time constraints:

$$L_{it} + N_{it} = \theta.$$

$$i = 1, 2;\ t = 1, 2, \ldots, T. \quad \text{(A1.5)}$$

Substitute the time constraints of equations (A1.5) into the budget constraint of equation (A1.4) to obtain

$$\sum_{t=1}^{T} R_t(p_t X_t + w_{1t} L_{1t} + w_{2t} L_{2t}) = W_0, \qquad \text{(A1.6)}$$

where W_0 is full wealth:

$$W_0 = \sum_{t=1}^{T} R_t(w_{1t}\theta + w_{2t}\theta) + A_0.$$

Finally, the non-negativity constraints are

$$\left.\begin{array}{l} L_{it},\, N_{it} \geq 0;\ i = 1, 2; \\[4pt] X_t \geq 0; \\[4pt] C_t \geq 0. \end{array}\right\} \quad t = 1, 2, \ldots, T. \quad \text{(A1.7)}$$

---

53. We assume that all expectations are fulfilled and that the utility function given below is consistent. Conditions for consistency have been examined by Robert H. Strotz, "Myopia and Inconsistency in Dynamic Utility Maximization," *Review of Economic Studies*, vol. 23 (1955–56), pp. 165–180.

The household is assumed to maximize its utility subject to the full-wealth constraint given by equation (A1.6). For the present the non-negativity constraints given by (A1.7) are assumed to be ineffective. We construct the Lagrangean function

$$\mathscr{L} = U(C_1, C_2, \ldots, C_t)$$

$$- \lambda \left[\sum_{t=1}^{T} R_t(p_t X_t + w_{1t} L_{1t} + w_{2t} L_{2t}) - W_0 \right]; \quad \text{(A1.8)}$$

and set its derivatives equal to zero:

$$\frac{\partial \mathscr{L}}{\partial X_t} = \frac{\partial U}{\partial C_t} \frac{\partial F}{\partial X_t} - \lambda R_t p_t = 0;$$

$$t = 1, 2, \ldots, T. \quad \text{(A1.9)}$$

$$\frac{\partial \mathscr{L}}{\partial L_{it}} = \frac{\partial U}{\partial C_t} \frac{\partial F}{\partial L_{it}} - \lambda R_t w_{it} = 0;$$

$$i = 1, 2; t = 1, 2, \ldots, T. \quad \text{(A1.10)}$$

$$\frac{\partial \mathscr{L}}{\partial \lambda} = \sum_{t=1}^{T} R_t(p_t X_t + w_{1t} L_{1t} + w_{2t} L_{2t}) - W_0 = 0. \quad \text{(A1.11)}$$

Since the marginal products of goods and times are positive, the equilibrium conditions given by equations (A1.9) and (A1.10) can be written equivalently as:

$$\frac{\partial U}{\partial C_t} = \lambda R_t \pi_t, \qquad t = 1, 2, \ldots, T. \quad \text{(A1.12)}$$

where

$$\pi_t = \frac{p_t}{\partial F/\partial X_t} = \frac{w_{1t}}{\partial F/\partial L_{1t}} = \frac{w_{2t}}{\partial F/\partial L_{2t}}.$$

$$t = 1, 2, \ldots, T. \quad \text{(A1.13)}$$

The conditions given by (A1.13) could be obtained by minimizing the total cost of producing C_t for a given level of C_t. π_t is, therefore, the marginal cost of commodities at age t. Correspondingly, the equilibrium conditions of (A1.12) could be obtained by minimizing the lifetime expenditures on commodities to attain a given level of utility.

From these cost-minimization conditions and the production function, we get the derived demand functions for goods and time:

$$X_t = X(w_{1t}, w_{2t}, p_t, C_t); \quad \text{(A1.14)}$$

$$L_{it} = L_i(w_{1t}, w_{2t}, p_t, C_t). \qquad i = 1, 2. \quad \text{(A1.15)}$$

Since these demand functions are homogeneous of degree zero in prices and homogeneous of the first degree in output, then

$$X_t = x(w_{1t}^*, w_{2t}^*)C_t; \tag{A1.16}$$

$$L_{it} = l_i(w_{it}^*, w_{2t}^*)C_t; \tag{A1.17}$$

where $w_{it}^* = w_{it}/p_t$, and $i = 1, 2$.

Changes in the derived demands for goods and times would depend on changes in the real wage rates and in the production of commodities.

Although none of the variables in a discrete-time model are differentiable functions of time, we can express the changes in the demand for goods and time in a simple form by using a linear expansion of a function around a point. Let $\tilde{x}_t = (x_{t+1} - x_t)/x_t$ for any variable x. Then

$$\tilde{X}_t = \eta_{x1}\tilde{w}_{1t}^* + \eta_{x2}\tilde{w}_{2t}^* + \tilde{C}_t; \tag{A1.18}$$

$$\tilde{L}_{it} = \eta_{i1}\tilde{w}_{1t}^* + \eta_{i2}\tilde{w}_{2t}^* + \tilde{C}_t; \qquad i = 1, 2. \tag{A1.19}$$

where η_{xj}, η_{ij} are the elasticities of demand for goods and for ith time at the jth wage rate, evaluated at the point (w_{1t}^*, w_{2t}^*), and holding output constant.

Since own substitution effects are negative, $\eta_{ii} < 0$, for $i = 1, 2$. Compensated cross-price elasticities between any two factors are positive or negative as these factors are substitutes or complements. The symmetry property of cross-substitution effects is more explicit with partial elasticities of substitution (PES). The PES σ_{ij} between the ith and jth time is defined by $\eta_{ij} = s_j\sigma_{ij}$, and the PES σ_{xj} between goods and the jth home time by $\eta_{xj} = s_j\sigma_{xj}$, where s_j is the proportion of jth time in the total cost of commodities. By symmetry, $\sigma_{ij} = \sigma_{ji}$ and $\sigma_{xj} = \sigma_{jx}$.

Substituting these expressions into (A1.18) and (A1.19) we get:

$$\tilde{X}_t = s_1\sigma_{x1}\tilde{w}_{1t}^* + s_2\sigma_{x2}\tilde{w}_{2t}^* + \tilde{C}_t; \tag{A1.20}$$

$$\tilde{L}_{it} = s_1\sigma_{i1}\tilde{w}_{1t}^* + s_2\sigma_{i2}\tilde{w}_{2t}^* + \tilde{C}_t. \qquad i = 1, 2. \tag{A1.21}$$

With the additive utility function given by (A1.3), the equilibrium conditions (A1.12) specialize to

$$\beta_t G'(C_t) = \lambda R_t \pi_t, \tag{A1.22}$$

or $G'(C_t) = \lambda\gamma_t$, with $\gamma_t = R_t\pi_t/\beta_t$. Solving for C_t, we obtain $C_t = C(\lambda\gamma_t)$, where $C(.)$ is the inverse of the function $G'(.)$, and λ, the marginal utility of wealth, is a constant over a lifetime in the absence of unexpected changes in prices and incomes. The change in consumption of commodities may be approximated up to first-order terms by

$$C_{t+1} - C_t = \frac{1}{G''} \lambda(\gamma_{t+1} - \gamma_t).$$

Substituting for λ from (A1.22) and dividing by C_t, we obtain

$$\tilde{C}_t = \frac{G'}{G''C_t} \tilde{\gamma}_t.$$

But $\tilde{\gamma}_t$ can be approximated by $\tilde{\pi}_t - r_t + \rho_t$, where $\rho_t = (\beta_{t+1} - \beta_t)/\beta_t$. Moreover, it can be shown that $-G'/G''C_t$ is equal to the direct (McFadden) elasticity of substitution σ_c between C_t and C_{t+1} evaluated at the point $C_{t+1} = C_t$. Hence,

$$\tilde{C}_t = -\sigma_c(\tilde{\pi}_t - r_t + \rho_t). \tag{A1.23}$$

To linear approximation, the change in marginal (= average) cost is given by

$$\tilde{\pi}_t = s_{1t}\tilde{w}_{1t} + s_{2t}\tilde{w}_{2t} + (1 - s_1 - s_2)\tilde{p}_t.$$

Hence,

$$\tilde{\pi}_t^* = s_{1t}\tilde{w}_{1t}^* + s_{2t}\tilde{w}_{2t}^*, \tag{A1.24}$$

where $\pi_t^* = \pi_t/p_t$. Therefore, by substituting (A1.24) into (A1.23),

$$\tilde{C}_t = -\sigma_c(s_{1t}\tilde{w}_{1t}^* + s_{2t}\tilde{w}_{2t}^* - r_t^* + \rho_t). \tag{A1.25}$$

Equation (A1.25) enables us to write the derived demands for goods and time as functions only of the interest rate net of time preference and of changes in real wage rates:

$$\tilde{X}_t = s_1(\sigma_{x1} - \sigma_c)\tilde{w}_{1t}^* + s_2(\sigma_{x2} - \sigma_c)\tilde{w}_{2t}^* + \sigma_c(r_t^* - \rho_t); \tag{A1.26}$$

and

$$\tilde{L}_{it} = s_1(\sigma_{i1} - \sigma_c)\tilde{w}_{1t}^* + s_2(\sigma_{i2} - \sigma_c)\tilde{w}_{2t}^* + \sigma_c(r_t^* - \rho_t).$$

$$i = 1, 2. \tag{A1.27}$$

Factor shares and elasticities of substitution need not be constant. Shares would be independent of wage rates if, and only if, all cross-partial elasticities of substitution in production equaled unity.[54]

2   CHANGES IN NONMARKET PRODUCTIVITY

We represent changes in productivity with age in the factor-augmenting form:

$$C_t = F(X_t, L_{1t}, L_{2t}; t) = F(a_{xt}X_t, a_{1t}L_{1t}, a_{2t}L_{2t}), \tag{A1.28}$$

and construct the same Lagrangean function as in (A1.8). If its derivatives are set equal to zero, the following result is obtained:

$$\frac{\partial U}{\partial C_t} = \lambda R_t \pi_t = 0; \tag{A1.29}$$

$$\pi_t = \frac{p_t/a_{xt}}{\partial F/\partial a_{xt}X_t} = \frac{w_{1t}/a_{1t}}{\partial F/\partial a_{1t}L_{1t}} = \frac{w_{2t}/a_{2t}}{\partial F/\partial a_{2t}L_{2t}}. \tag{A1.30}$$

---

54. Indeed,

$$\tilde{s}_{it} = s_{xt}(1 - \sigma_{ix})\tilde{w}_{it}^* + s_{jt}(1 - \sigma_{ij})(\tilde{w}_{it}^* - \tilde{w}_{jt}^*). \qquad i, j = L_1, L_2; j \neq i.$$

The derived demand for goods and time are now:

$$a_{xt}X_t = X(w_{1t}/a_{1t}, w_{2t}/a_{2t}, p_t/a_{xt})C_t; \tag{A1.31}$$

$$a_{it}L_{it} = L_i(w_{1t}/a_{1t}, w_{2t}/a_{2t}, p_t/a_{xt})C_t. \qquad i = 1, 2. \tag{A1.32}$$

Therefore, the percentage changes in X and L are

$$\tilde{X}_t = -\tilde{a}_{xt} + s_1\sigma_{x1}(\tilde{W}_{1t} - \tilde{a}_{1t}) + s_2\sigma_{xt}(\tilde{W}_{2t} - \tilde{a}_{2t}) + s_x\sigma_{xx}(\tilde{p}_t - \tilde{a}_{xt}) + \tilde{C}_t; \tag{A1.33}$$

$$\tilde{L}_{it} = -\tilde{a}_{it} + s_1\sigma_{i1}(\tilde{W}_{1t} - \tilde{a}_{1t}) + s_2\sigma_{i2}(\tilde{W}_{2t} - \tilde{a}_{2t}) + s_x\sigma_{ix}(\tilde{p}_t - \tilde{a}_{xt}) + \tilde{C}_t.$$

$$i = 1, 2. \tag{A1.34}$$

Equation (A1.23) still holds, since a change in productivity affects the consumption of commodities only through variations in their prices. However, the price changes are now given by

$$\tilde{\pi}_t = s_1(\tilde{W}_{1t} - \tilde{a}_{1t}) + s_2(\tilde{W}_{2t} - \tilde{a}_{2t}) + s_x(\tilde{p}_t - \tilde{a}_{xt}). \tag{A1.35}$$

A substitution of (A1.35) and (A1.23) into (A1.33) and (A1.34) yields the following results:

$$\tilde{X}_t = -\tilde{a}_{xt} + s_1\sigma_{x1}(\tilde{W}_{1t} - \tilde{a}_{1t}) + s_2\sigma_{x2}(\tilde{W}_{2t} - \tilde{a}_{2t}) + s_x\sigma_{xx}(\tilde{p}_t - \tilde{a}_{2t})$$
$$- \sigma_c[s_1(\tilde{W}_{1t} - \tilde{a}_{1t}) + s_2(\tilde{W}_{2t} - \tilde{a}_{2t}) + s_x(\tilde{p}_t - \tilde{a}_{xt}) - r_t^* + \rho_t]; \tag{A1.36}$$

$$L_{it} = -\tilde{a}_{it} + s_1\sigma_{i1}(\tilde{W}_{1t} - \tilde{a}_{1t}) + s\sigma_{i2}(\tilde{W}_{2t} - \tilde{a}_{2t}) + s_x\sigma_{ix}(\tilde{p}_t - \tilde{a}_{xt})$$
$$- \sigma_c[s_1(\tilde{W}_{1t} - \tilde{a}_{1t}) + s_2(\tilde{W}_{2t} - \tilde{a}_{2t}) + s_x(\tilde{p}_t - \tilde{a}_{xt}) - r_t^* + \rho_t];$$

$$i = 1, 2. \tag{A1.37}$$

or, by regrouping terms,

$$\tilde{X}_t = (\sigma_{x1} - \sigma_c)s_1(\tilde{W}_{1t} - \tilde{p}_t) + (\sigma_{x2} - \sigma_c)s_2(\tilde{W}_{2t} - \tilde{p}_t) + (\sigma_c - 1)\hat{F}_t$$
$$+ (1 - \sigma_{x1})s_1(\tilde{a}_{1t} - \tilde{a}_{xt}) + (1 - \sigma_{x2})s_2(\tilde{a}_{2t} - \tilde{a}_{xt}) + \sigma_c(r_t - \tilde{p}_t - \rho_t); \tag{A1.38}$$

$$L_{it} = (\sigma_{i1} - \sigma_c)s_1(\tilde{W}_{1t} - \tilde{p}_t) + (\sigma_{i2} - \sigma_c)s_2(\tilde{W}_{2t} - \tilde{p}_t) + (\sigma_c - 1)\hat{F}_t$$
$$+ (1 - \sigma_{ij})s_j(\tilde{a}_{jt} - \tilde{a}_{it}) + (1 - \sigma_{ix})s_x(\tilde{a}_{xt} - \tilde{a}_{it}) + \sigma_i - \tilde{p}_t - \rho_t);$$

$$i, j = 1, 2; \ j \neq i. \tag{A1.39}$$

where $\hat{F}_t = s_1\tilde{a}_{1t} + s_2\tilde{a}_{2t} + s_x\tilde{a}_{xt}$ is the percentage increase in the output of commodities at constant factor inputs, or the percentage reduction in their marginal cost, due to the increase in productivity.

3   PRODUCTION OF HUMAN CAPITAL

I now permit the accumulation of human capital, and introduce the following additional notation:

H_{it} = stock of human capital held by the ith family member at age t of the household head;

h_{it} = rate of production of human capital by the ith member at age t;

N'_{it} = amount of time spent by the ith member in producing human capital at age t;

X'_{it} = amount of goods used by the ith member in producing human capital at age t;

δ_{it} = rate of depreciation of human capital of the ith member at age t;

$D_{iv,t}$ = undepreciated portion at age t of one unit of the ith member's human capital held at v:

$$D_{iv,t} = (1 - \delta_{iv})(1 - \delta_{iv+1}) \ldots (1 - \delta_{it-1}).$$

$$i = 1, 2; \ v = 1, 2, \ldots, t - 1$$

It is assumed here that only wage rates depend on the stock of human capital, as in

$$w_{it} = e_{it}H_{it}. \qquad i = 1, 2. \quad \text{(A1.40)}$$

In the text I also consider briefly the effects of human capital on the productivity of goods and time in the production of commodities and human capital itself. The initial stocks H_{i1} are given, but later stocks depend on the amounts produced and not depreciated:

$$H_{it} = H_i D_{i1,t} + \sum_{v=1}^{t-1} h_{iv} D_{i,v,t}; \qquad i = 1, 2. \quad \text{(A1.41)}$$

with [55]

$$h_{it} = h_i(X'_{it}, N'_{it}).$$

$$i = 1, 2; \ t = 1, 2, \ldots, T. \quad \text{(A1.42)}$$

The time constraints are

$$L_{it} + N_{it} + N'_{it} = \theta;$$

$$i = 1, 2; \ t = 1, 2, \ldots, T. \quad \text{(A1.43)}$$

and the budget constraint is

$$\sum_{t=1}^{T} R_t(p_t X_t + p'_{1t}X'_{1t} + p'_{2t}X_{2t}) = \sum_{t=1}^{T} R_t(e_{1t}H_{1t}N_{1t} + e_{2t}H_{2t}N_{2t}) + A_0. \quad \text{(A1.44)}$$

If the derivatives of the Lagrangean function,

$$\mathscr{L} = U(C_1, C_2, \ldots, C_t) - \lambda \left[\sum_{t=1}^{T} R_t(p_t X_t + p'_t X'_t - e_{1t}H_{1t}N_{1t} - e_{2t}H_{2t}N_{2t}) - A_0 \right]$$

$$- \sum_{t=1}^{T} \sum_{i=1}^{2} \kappa_{it}(L_{it} + N_{it} + N'_{it} - \theta),$$

---

55. Interactions between husband and wife in the production function for human capital are ignored here, but could easily be introduced.

are set equal to zero, then

$$\frac{\partial \mathcal{L}}{\partial X_t} = \frac{\partial U}{\partial C_t} \frac{\partial F}{\partial X_t} - \lambda R_t p_t = 0; \tag{A1.45}$$

$$\frac{\partial \mathcal{L}}{\partial L_{it}} = \frac{\partial U}{\partial C_t} \frac{\partial F}{\partial L_{it}} - \kappa_{it} = 0; \qquad i = 1, 2. \tag{A1.46}$$

$$\frac{\partial \mathcal{L}}{\partial N_{it}} = \lambda R_t e_{it} H_{it} - \kappa_{it} = 0; \qquad i = 1, 2. \tag{A1.47}$$

$$\frac{\partial \mathcal{L}}{\partial N'_{it}} = \lambda \left(\sum_{v=t+1}^{T} R_v e_{iv} N_{iv} \frac{\partial H_{iv}}{\partial h_{it}} \frac{\partial h_{it}}{\partial N'_{it}} \right) - \kappa_{it} = 0;$$

$$i = 1, 2. \tag{A1.48}$$

$$\frac{\partial \mathcal{L}}{\partial X'_{it}} = \lambda \left(\sum_{v=t+1}^{T} R_v e_{iv} N_{iv} \frac{\partial H_{iv}}{\partial h_{it}} \frac{\partial h_{it}}{\partial X'_{it}} - R_t p'_t \right) = 0;$$

$$i = 1, 2. \tag{A1.49}$$

where λ can be interpreted as the marginal utility of wealth, and κ_{it} as the marginal utility of the ith member's time at age t of the household head.

From (A1.47), it is seen that the monetary equivalent of the marginal utility of time is equal to the wage rate. Therefore, (A1.45) and (A1.46) may be rewritten as

$$\frac{\partial U}{\partial C_t} = \lambda R_t \pi_t; \tag{A1.50}$$

$$\pi_t = \frac{p_t}{\partial F / \partial X_t} = \frac{e_{1t} H_{1t}}{\partial F / \partial L_{it}} = \frac{e_{2t} H_{2t}}{\partial F / \partial L_{2t}}. \tag{A1.51}$$

Moreover, the equilibrium conditions (A1.48) and (A1.49) may be written as

$$\sum_{v=t+1}^{T} R_v e_{iv} N_{iv} \frac{\partial H_{iv}}{\partial h_{it}} = R_t \mu_{it}; \tag{A1.52}$$

$$R_t \mu_{it} = \frac{\kappa_{it}/\lambda}{\partial h / \partial N'_{it}} = \frac{R_t p'_t}{\partial h / \partial X'_{it}}; \tag{A1.53}$$

where μ_{it} is the "current" marginal cost of producing the ith member's human capital at age t of the household head. The "full" marginal cost includes the increase in future total costs attributable to the effects on future wage rates of an additional unit produced at age t.

Let $K_{it} = K_i(e_{it} H_{it}, p'_t, h_{it})$ denote total costs of producing the ith member's human capital at age t. Then the optimality conditions (A1.52) may be expressed as

$$\sum_{v=t+1}^{T} R_v e_{iv} \theta'_{iv} \frac{\partial H_{iv}}{\partial h_{iv}} = R_t \frac{\partial K_{it}}{\partial h_{it}} + \sum_{v=t+1}^{T} R_v e_{iv} \frac{\partial K_{iv}}{\partial e_{iv} H_{iv}} \frac{\partial H_{iv}}{\partial h_{it}}; \tag{A1.54}$$

where the right-hand side is full marginal cost, with $\partial K_{iv}/\partial e_{iv}H_{iv} = N'_{iv}$. The first term on the right-hand side measures current marginal cost, whereas the second measures the discounted value of the increment in future costs of producing human capital due to a small rise in the rate of output in period t. The left-hand side is "full" benefits, since θ'_{iv} is the market time of the ith household member at time v: $\theta'_{iv} = N_{iv} + N'_{iv}$. If full benefits were independent of the amount produced, second-order conditions would require only that full marginal costs be an increasing function of h_t:

$$R_t \frac{\partial^2 K_{it}}{\partial h_{it}^2} + \sum_{v=t+1}^{T} R_v \frac{\partial^2 K_{iv}}{\partial H_{iv}^2} \frac{\partial H_{iv}}{\partial h_{it}} > 0.$$

A fortiori, full marginal cost must be increasing in h_t if full marginal benefits are positively related to the rate of output of human capital. Since consumption and investment decisions are determined simultaneously, consumption time will fall as the cost of time increases through increased production of human capital. Market time, θ', and thus full marginal benefits will be positively related to the output of human capital in previous periods.

2

The Allocation of Goods
Over the Life Cycle [1]

2.1   PRELIMINARIES

The purpose of the empirical work reported in this chapter is to explain consumption behavior over the life cycle. The model developed in Chapter 1 predicted some systematic relationships between a household's consumption of goods (and time) and the wage rates of its earners over their lifetime. My task now will be to develop an empirical methodology capable of capturing these life cycle effects.

In Chapter 1 it was shown in particular that the change in the demand for goods at age t is:

$$\tilde{X}_t = b_1 \tilde{w}_{1t}^* + b_2 \tilde{w}_{2t}^* + b_z \tilde{Z}_t + b_t; \qquad (2.1)$$

with

$$b_1 = (\sigma_{x1} - \sigma_c)s_1;$$

$$b_2 = (\sigma_{x2} - \sigma_c)s_2;$$

$$b_z = (\sigma_c - 1)\epsilon;$$

$$b_t = \sigma_c(r_t^* - \rho_t);$$

NOTE: Ghez is solely responsible for this chapter.
1. I am grateful to Barry Geller for helpful computational assistance.

where

t = age of household head;

$\tilde{X}_t$ = percentage change in the consumption of market goods at age t;

$\bar{w}_{1t}^*, \bar{w}_{2t}^*$ = percentage change in the real wage rate of husband (subscript 1) and wife (subscript 2) at age t;

$\tilde{Z}_t$ = percentage change in some characteristic or environmental variable Z that governs nonmarket productivity;

r_t^* = real rate of interest at age t;

ρ_t = rate of time preference at age t;

σ_{x1}, σ_{x2} = partial elasticities of substitution between goods and husband's and wife's home time;

σ_c = elasticity of substitution between commodities in period t and commodities in period $t+1$;

s_1, s_2 = shares of husband's and wife's time in total costs of commodities at age t;

ϵ = elasticity of response of nonmarket productivity to a 1 per cent change in the environmental variable Z.

Equation (2.1) could be used directly as an estimating equation if the following four conditions were met: (i) if household expectations were in fact fulfilled; (ii) if complete life histories of households were available; (iii) if changes in nonmarket productivity could be related to some observable determinants called Z; (iv) if the elasticities b_1, b_2, b_z, and b_t were constant.

These conditions are hard to meet. Since perfect foresight, for one, is an unreasonable assumption, I formulate a more plausible expectations model in the next section.

In the second place, reinterview data are scarce and incomplete. In section 3, therefore, I develop a procedure for testing life cycle behavior with cross-sectional data.

Third, observable determinants of nonmarket productivity are difficult to come by with existing data. I shall assume henceforth that increases in family size are either the source or are highly correlated with factors that raise productivity in the home.

In the development of an estimating equation, I shall also assume that the elasticities b_1, b_2, b_z, and b_t in equation (2.1) are all constant. In other words, I assume that the rate of interest net of time preference, the elasticities of substitution in production [2] and in consumption, and factor shares are all constant. The validity of the assumption of constant factor shares is tested in Chapter 4.[3]

2.2   AN EXPECTATIONS MODEL

Suppose that household anticipations were not fully realized. What would be the effect of these errors on the consumption path? Consider first the substitution of goods for home time. Since we assumed that the production function is homogeneous of the first degree, factor proportions in production at any age depend only on the real wage rates and on the shape of the production function at that age. Goods intensity of production is independent of commodity output and therefore of all future variables. Since actual changes in factor proportions at any age depend on the actual change in factor prices at that age, they are independent of whether expectations are fulfilled or not.[4]

By contrast, the absolute level of consumption of goods at any age t depends on expectations held at that age, because the absolute amount of commodity consumption at t depends on estimated full wealth at t and on anticipated prices.

Thus, if price or income expectations were not fulfilled, the actual change in goods and commodity consumption would be governed not only by substitution effects, as explained in Chapter 1, but also by wealth effects.

To give a more formal presentation, I shall suppose that elas-

---

2. Subject to a minor qualification, if partial elasticities of substitution are constant they are necessarily equal, i.e., $\sigma_{x1} = \sigma_{x2} = \sigma_{12}$. See Hirofumi Uzawa, "Production Functions with Constant Elasticities of Substitution," *Review of Economic Studies* (October 1962), pp. 291–299.

3. The factor shares s_1 and s_2 would not in general be constant if the elasticities of substitution in production were not unity.

4. This implication is no longer true if there are costs of adjustment associated with inputs. In the short run the stock of durable goods is fixed for each household. Therefore, unanticipated changes in real income give rise to diminishing returns in the use of household time, and generate induced substitution effects away from commodities produced with fixed stocks of durable goods. Further developments are contained in Gilbert R. Ghez, "Life Cycle Demand for Consumer Durable Goods" (unpublished, 1968).

ticities of substitution in consumption are constant and equal.[5] The actual change in commodity consumption of a given household at age t of the head is

$$\tilde{C}_t = (\hat{W}_t^* - \hat{P}_t^*) - \sigma_c(\tilde{\pi}_t^* - \hat{P}_t^*) + \sigma_c(r_t^* - \rho_t); \qquad (2.2)$$

where

$\tilde{\pi}_t^*$ = the *actual* percentage change in the price of commodities at age t;

$\hat{W}_t^*$ = the *unanticipated* percentage change in full wealth at t;

$\hat{P}_t^*$ = the *unanticipated* percentage change at t in a price index of current and future commodities.

If all future prices and incomes were prefectly predicted, the actual change in commodity consumption at age t would be simply $\tilde{C}_t = -\sigma_c \tilde{\pi}_t^* + \sigma_c(r^* - \rho)$, as developed in Chapter 1. The introduction of unexpected changes has in general two effects:

i. It introduces wealth effects on consumption. The unexpected change in real wealth is $\hat{W}^* - \hat{P}^*$, and this creates a percentage change of $\hat{W}^* - \hat{P}^*$ in commodity consumption, since the wealth elasticity of consumption has been assumed to equal unity, as explained in note 5.

ii. It affects the actual amount of substitution in consumption, since the relevant change in relative prices is $\tilde{\pi}^* - \hat{P}^*$ rather than $\tilde{\pi}^*$ alone.

For instance, an unexpectedly high wage rate at age t, whether or not it is accompanied by an upward revision of future wage expectations, raises full wealth. It also raises the value of the price index. As long as hours of work are positive, full wealth would rise more than the price index, and therefore real wealth would increase.[6]

---

5. Notice that if the utility function is additively separable and has constant elasticities of substitution, it is necessarily homogeneous. Wealth elasticities of consumption are equal to unity. For a proof, see Daniel McFadden, "Constant Elasticity of Substitution Production Functions," *Review of Economic Studies* (June 1963), pp. 73–83.

6. We would have

$$\hat{W}_t^* = \sum_{t'=t}^{T} (\alpha_{1t't}\hat{w}_{1t't}^* + \alpha_{2t't}\hat{w}_{2t't}^*);$$

$$\hat{P}_t^* = \sum_{t'=t}^{T} k_{t't}(s_{1t't}\hat{w}_{1t't}^* + s_{2t't}\hat{w}_{2t't}^*);$$

where

Over its life cycle, a household could be underestimating its real wealth at certain times and overestimating it at others. Therefore, if households were taken as units of observation, wealth and substitution effects could be sorted out only if a direct measure of estimated wealth were available or if a relationship could be established between expectations and past realizations.

Yet, if we consider a group of households whose permanent characteristics are the same, it is plausible that some households overestimate, while other households underestimate, their future incomes, their future market and nonmarket efficiency, and their life span. I shall suppose that on the average expectations are fulfilled. In other words, if all households that are homogeneous in such permanent characteristics as schooling and race are grouped by year of age, the average unexpected change in full wealth and in the price index is assumed to equal zero. Let there be n homogeneous households; then

$$\sum_{i=1}^{n} \hat{W}_{it}^{*} = 0; \qquad\qquad t = 1, 2, \ldots, T.$$

(2.3)

$$\sum_{i=1}^{n} \hat{P}_{it}^{*} = 0. \qquad\qquad t = 1, 2, \ldots, T.$$

$\hat{w}_{it't}^{*}$ = percentage revision, at age t of the household, of the ith member's wage rate expectation at age t';

$\alpha_{it't}$ = ratio of the ith member's (estimated) discounted full earnings at age t' to household full wealth (estimated) at age t;

$k_{t't}$ = discounted estimated share of commodities at age t' in family full wealth (estimated) at age t.

Therefore,

$$\alpha_{it't} - k_{t't}s_{it't} = \frac{R_{t't}^{*}w_{it't}N_{it't}}{W_{t-1}^{*}}.$$

Actually equation (2.2) is sufficiently general to accommodate the effects of mistaken expectations and revisions of future expectations not only about wage rates, but also about nonwage income, nonmarket efficiency, interest rates, and the life span. An unexpectedly high nonwage income, a windfall, raises real wealth by raising full wealth, while an unexpected increase in nonmarket efficiency raises real wealth by reducing the value of the price index. An unexpectedly low rate of interest at time t raises or reduces real wealth according as the household is a net borrower or a net lender at that particular time. An upward revision in life expectancy raises full wealth as long as the extra years are not all spent in retirement; since it also increases the number of periods over which wealth is to be allocated, current consumption would rise or fall according as the extra earnings were greater or smaller than the consumption of goods during the extra years of life.

Since within-cohort expectations are unbiased, changes in cohort consumption are governed by substitution effects alone. For the hth homogeneous group we have:

$$\tilde{C}_{ht} = -\sigma_c \tilde{\pi}_{ht}^* + \sigma_c(r^* - \rho)$$

$$= -\sigma_c(s_1 \tilde{w}_{1ht}^* + s_2 \tilde{w}_{2ht}^*) + \sigma_c \epsilon \tilde{Z}_{ht} + \sigma_c(r^* - \rho); \tag{2.4}$$

and

$$\tilde{X}_{ht} = (\sigma_{x1} - \sigma_c)s_1 \tilde{w}_{1ht}^* + (\sigma_{x2} - \sigma_c)s_2 \tilde{w}_{2ht}^* + (\sigma_c - 1)\epsilon \tilde{Z}_{ht} + \sigma_c(r^* - \rho); \tag{2.5}$$

where the subscripts ht denote the geometric mean of a variable over all households within group h at age t of the household head.

2.3 TRENDS IN REAL WEALTH

As I mentioned in section 2.1, no systematic reinterview data are available. I proceed now to show how the model can be tested with cross-sectional data.

In a cross section, households differ in their real wealth. If, for a given cohort, all households that are homogeneous in permanent characteristics such as schooling and race are grouped by age of head, average real wealth would be independent of age, as indicated in the expectations model described in section 2.2. But even for homogeneous groups, average real wealth varies *across* cohorts. Hence, in a cross section, average real wealth is expected to vary with age. Since real wage rates are growing over time, younger schooling- and race-specific cohorts have higher real wealth than comparable older ones. Similarly, if average household productivity is rising over time, the absolute price of commodities will fall over time and real wealth will rise.

More formally, we have

$$\dot{C}_{ht} = (\dot{W}_{ht}^* - \dot{P}_{ht}^*) - \sigma_c(\dot{\pi}_{ht}^* - \dot{P}_{ht}^*) + \sigma_c(r^* - \rho); \tag{2.6}$$

where the dot above a variable denotes the percentage difference in that variable for a one-year difference in age in the cross section, and

$$\dot{X}_{ht} = \dot{W}_{ht} - (1 - \sigma_c)\dot{P}_{ht} + (\sigma_{x1} - \sigma_c)s_1 \dot{W}_{1ht}$$

$$+ (\sigma_{x2} - \sigma_c)s_2 \dot{W}_{2ht} + (\sigma_c - 1)\epsilon \dot{Z}_{ht} + \sigma_c(r^* - \rho). \tag{2.7}$$

If growth in market productivity is age-neutral and occurs at a constant rate g_w for both husband and wife, in the sense that it raises the wages of both at a constant rate g_w regardless of age, and if nonmarket productivity growth occurs at the constant rate of g_f, then [7] $-\dot{W}_{ht} = g_w$; and $-\dot{P}_{ht} = (s_1 + s_2)g_w - g_f$. Hence,

$$\dot{X}_{ht} = b_1\dot{w}_{1ht} + b_2\dot{w}_{2ht} + b_2\dot{Z}_{ht} + b_t; \tag{2.8}$$

where b_1, b_2, and b_z are defined as for cohort behavior [see equation (2.1)], but where b_t now includes not only the effects of the interest rate and of time preference but also the effects of trends in market and nonmarket efficiency: [8]

$$b_t = \sigma_c(r^* - \rho) - [(1 - s_1 - s_2) + \sigma_c(s_1 + s_2)]g_w - (1 - \sigma_c)g_f.$$

If we integrate equation (2.8) we get the appropriate consumption function for the cross section:

$$\log X_{ht} = b_0 + b_1 \log w_{1ht} + b_2 \log w_{2ht} + b_z \log Z_{ht} + b_t t; \tag{2.9}$$

where b_0 is an indicator of real wealth of the youngest cohort in the cross section. In principle, life cycle consumption behavior could be estimated from a single cross section by using equation (2.8) or (2.9). From a relatively complex model rather simple estimating equations have been generated.

For the actual empirical computations reported in the next several sections, these equations had to be modified somewhat, because of data limitations, which I discuss in more detail below. In particular, I use annual earnings to measure wage rates, and I assume that there are no differences among cohorts in nonmarket efficiency.[9]

---

7. If factor shares were not constant, $\dot{P}$ would also depend on the covariance between the budget shares, k, of consumption in full income and the combined share of husband's and wife's time, $s_1 + s_2$.

8. In the same manner, one can derive equations for consumption time appropriate for the cross section:

$$\dot{L}_{iht} = a_{i1}\dot{w}_{1ht} + a_{i2}\dot{w}_{2ht} + a_{iz}\dot{Z}_{ht} + a_{it}. \qquad i = 1, 2.$$

Since the production function is homogeneous,

$$a_{it} = b_t; \quad i = 1, 2.$$

In Chapter 3, Becker uses this methodology to estimate the demand for time by men.

9. A simultaneous equation bias is introduced because earnings and consumption are jointly determined in the model. Instrumental variables estimation techniques would have been more appropriate than ordinary least squares.

2.4   THE DATA

The main data source [10] used is the Survey of Consumer Expenditures for 1960–61, conducted by the Bureau of Labor Statistics.[11] This is a nationwide survey of family expenditure, income, and several personal characteristics of 13,728 households. The survey covers the two years 1960 and 1961. Observations from both periods were retained in order not to reduce the sample size inordinately.

Households were cross-classified in the following ways:[12]

i. By age of household head: 44 age groups by single year of age of the head, ranging from age 22 up to age 65.

ii. By education of the household head: level I: 0–8 years of schooling; level II: 9–12 years of schooling; level III: 13 or more years of schooling.

Age 22 was chosen as the lower bound because below that age the cells were often very small in size and because it is appropriate to delete those years of age in which many household heads (and their spouses) are pursuing full-time schooling.[13] Age 65 was chosen as the upper bound because in many households earners beyond that age are retired.[14]

Households were classified by schooling in order to verify whether or not life cycle patterns differ among households that differ in some permanent characteristic.[15] Households with a higher level

10. An auxiliary source used is the 1/1,000 sample of the U.S. population in 1960 (see Chapter 3, note 36, below). Some of the results which I obtained from pooling the BLS Survey with the 1/1,000 sample are reported in Chapter 4.

11. For a detailed description, see *Consumer Expenditures and Income: Survey Guidelines,* BLS Bull. 1684, 1971. See also Helen H. Lamale, *Methodology of the Survey of Consumer Expenditures in 1950* (Philadelphia: University of Pennsylvania, 1959).

12. The General Purpose Tapes created by the BLS were used, rather than the tabulated data. The latter give mean expenditures and income by age of family head, but with intervals of ten years of age. Moreover, family income by source is not classified by age.

13. Indeed, under those conditions, the price of time would be measured by the discounted value of marginal returns to schooling, rather than by the potential wage rate. See Chapter 1.

14. In the BLS Survey of Consumer Expenditures, the proportion of retired persons rises from 10 per cent at age 62, to 21 per cent at age 65, 37 per cent at age 66, 46 per cent at age 67, and exceeds 50 per cent starting with age 69.

15. A sorting of households by race as well as schooling would have been undertaken had nonwhite cells been sufficiently large. But the mean cell size for nonwhites between ages 22 and 65 is 16.6 for education level I, 12.1 for level II, and 2.9 for level III, with many empty or small cells.

of education are expected to have a very different consumption pattern than households with less education. In the first place, after completion of school the potential wage rate of the former group is higher, thereby inducing substitution toward the consumption of goods. Second, higher-educated people may have a higher level of real wealth because they are more able or because they have easier access to funds to finance their investments. This difference in lifetime real income would imply that the higher the level of education, the higher the consumption profile. According to the model developed in Chapter 1, the shape of the consumption profile would depend largely on the shape of the wage profile. The responsiveness of consumption to the wage rate over the life cycle would depend on (i) the importance of time in household production and (ii) substitution elasticities. This responsiveness would be the same at all levels of education if factor shares and elasticities of substitution did not differ by level of education. The higher wage rates of the more educated imply a substitution toward goods, but the factor shares would still be the same for all levels of education if the elasticity of substitution in production was equal to unity. In other words, the responsiveness of consumption to changes in the wage rate over the life cycle need not differ by level of schooling. This is a question that empirical estimation can resolve.

As shown in Table 2.1, the mean cell size is largest for education level II, i.e., for those households whose heads have completed nine to 12 years of schooling. The range of cell size across observations is wide: cell sizes are largest during the central years of life and taper off at the extremes.

Within each cell, I constructed the arithmetic means of certain

TABLE 2.1
CELL SIZES IN THE BLS SURVEY OF CONSUMER EXPENDITURES, 1960–61, FOR HOUSEHOLD HEAD OF AGES 22 TO 65

| | Number of Households | |
Education Level	Mean	Range
All	256.6	112–337
I (0–8 years)	83.7	11–145
II (9–12 years)	118.2	50–145
III (13 years or more)	54.7	19–89

variables.[16] Arithmetic means were used rather than the more appropriate geometric ones because the latter involve an obvious computational defect when zero values are encountered. In addition, the use of arithmetic means facilitates comparisons with other studies. Presumably this change of variable is not a source of much bias: under fairly general conditions the results are not affected at all.[17]

As my basic measure of consumption I took the sum of: (i) expenditures on nondurable goods and services;[18] (ii) the imputed value of housing services plus expenses for automobile operation; (iii) gifts.

For the model developed in Chapter 1, it was assumed that all goods are nondurable. To incorporate durable goods into the model, I suppose that their services enter the production function for commodities, along with nondurables and home time. As long as the price of the services of durable goods relative to the price of nondurables is constant over time, the sum of the value of the services of durables and nondurables would form a composite good whose behavior would depend on the real wage.

The BLS survey data are not adequate for calculating the value of the services of many durable goods. For housing, I estimated the average implicit rental of owners within each cell by the average rent paid by renters in the corresponding cell. This procedure is based on the assumption that capital markets are perfect, that there are no transactions costs associated with rentals or purchases, and that holders of durable goods are perfectly indifferent between ownership and rental of these goods. For automobiles, I included expenses for automobile operation in my measure of consumption on the assumption that these are proportional to the services of automobiles.

For other durable goods, such as house furnishings and durable recreation goods, no adjustment was possible. Hence, my measure of consumption understates true consumption. The underestimate

---

16. Since the Survey of Consumer Expenditures is a stratified sample, I used weighted means, using the reported survey weights. For the small-city stratum the weights for individual households were not reported by the BLS in order to preserve the anonymity of the respondents. Households in that stratum were weighted by the average weight of the stratum.

17. See the appendix to this chapter.

18. This is the BLS category "expenditures on current consumption" minus purchases of durable goods reported in the survey (purchases of furnishings and equipment, automobiles, TVs, radios, and musical instruments) minus expenses on owned dwelling.

would be relatively small at early years of age, if at the outset of the life cycle, initial stocks of durable goods were below their optimum levels. Some evidence of this condition is seen in the pattern of net investment in durable goods in the BLS Survey of Consumer Expenditures: net investment in durable goods rises at early ages, reaching a peak in the late twenties, then gradually declining and turning negative in the late sixties. Therefore, total true consumption would rise more rapidly at least initially than a measure of consumption that excluded the services of durable goods.

Gifts are included in my measure of consumption since these are a form of expenditure and the model of derived demand developed in Chapter 1 can be presumed to apply to them as well. Expenditures on property insurance are included, but not expenditures on personal insurance.

The Survey of Consumer Expenditures covers annual earnings of each household during the survey year, but does not contain information on hours of work and wage rates of each family member separately. As a measure of the price of time, I used family earnings plus self-employment income.[19] A full justification for the use of family earnings as a measure of the price of time is given in the appendix to this chapter. In brief, if the wife's wage rate is relatively steady over the life cycle (barring growth in real wages), as in fact it seems to be,[20] variations in her yearly earnings will basically reflect variations in her hours of work resulting from changes in the husband's wage rate (and from changes in nonmarket productivity). Her earnings will rise as his wage rate rises if his and her time are either complementary or not very strong substitutes. Moreover, his yearly earnings will rise as his wage rate rises.[21] Hence, family earnings will be positively related to his wage rate, as long as the correlation between his and her earnings is positive or not strongly negative.[22]

---

19. These are before-tax earnings. No attempt was made to correct for the progressivity of the income tax.

20. See in particular James Smith, "The Life Cycle Allocation of Time in a Family Context" (University of Chicago: Ph.D. diss., 1972). In his data from the Survey of Economic Opportunity, 1967, men's wages fluctuate over a much wider range than women's.

21. In this discussion I exclude interest rate and time preference effects.

22. One difficulty is that changes in wife's earnings reflect also changes in her (and his) nonmarket productivity. Therefore, changes in family earnings would also reflect these life cycle changes. For instance, if nonmarket effects were neutral across

No data exist on interest rates by age of head. However, as explained above, as long as interest rates are the same at all years of age, their effect on consumption is incorporated in the effect of age of head.

No direct measures of nonmarket productivity exist. I shall suppose that within each education group, production functions are the same for all cohorts in the cross section. In other words, at any particular time, the benefits of technological change in the household sector are spread over all households having the same level of education.

Other variables also retained from the BLS survey were family size and total family income.

The cross-sectional patterns of mean consumption and mean earnings by age of head are displayed in Figures 2.1, 2.2, and 2.3.

The curves in Figure 2.1 portray over-all mean earnings and consumption by age of head for all education levels combined. As predicted by the theory, earnings tend to rise initially, reach a peak in the mid- or late forties, and then decline. The rise and subsequent decline in earnings is presumably due not only to the rise and fall in wage rates, but also to the rise and fall in hours of work. Consumption distinctly follows the same path as earnings, rising initially, peaking at about age 45, and falling thereafter. It is important to note, however, that the consumption profile is less steep than the earnings profile: its initial rise is gentler, and its fall less rapid, than that of earnings, with earnings falling below consumption at about age 65. This smoothing of the income stream is an implication of the model developed in Chapter 1, although the point was not discussed there. If substitution in production is easier than in consumption, and the rate of interest net of time preference is close to zero, consumption will rise as wage rates and earnings rise, and fall as they fall. When consumption equals annual earnings its rate of change must be smaller (in absolute value) than that of earnings because if commodity output were constant (say because $\sigma_c = 0$), consumption of goods would rise more gently than earnings when the wage rate rose; a fortiori, this would occur if commodity output fell when the

---

factors, and if the elasticity of substitution in consumption was smaller than unity, improvements in home productivity would induce all family members to increase their hours of work and thus family earnings.

FIGURE 2.1
FAMILY CONSUMPTION AND EARNINGS BY AGE OF HEAD,
ALL EDUCATION LEVELS COMBINED

● Earnings
X Consumption

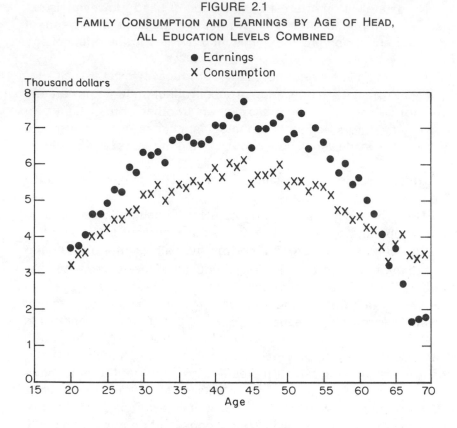

wage rate rose because of commodity substitution.[23] As noted above, this smoothing of income is observed in the data, which thereby provide some support to the model.

Households in each successively higher level of schooling have earnings profiles higher than those in the levels below (Figure 2.2). Their earnings tend to rise more rapidly and for a longer period of time. This is precisely what one would expect if on-the-job training were positively related to schooling. The consumption of households

---

23. For proof, notice that earnings E net of consumption X are equal to full earnings net of expenditures on household commodities: $E - X = wT - \pi C$. The rate of change of expenditures on commodities is (neglecting effects of interest rates and time preferences) $(1 - \sigma_c)s\bar{w} < \bar{w}$ for all values of $\sigma_c \geqslant 0$, since s (the combined share of household labor) is smaller than unity.

A slight modification in the argument is required if male and female wage rates grow at different rates, and if the production of human capital is considered.

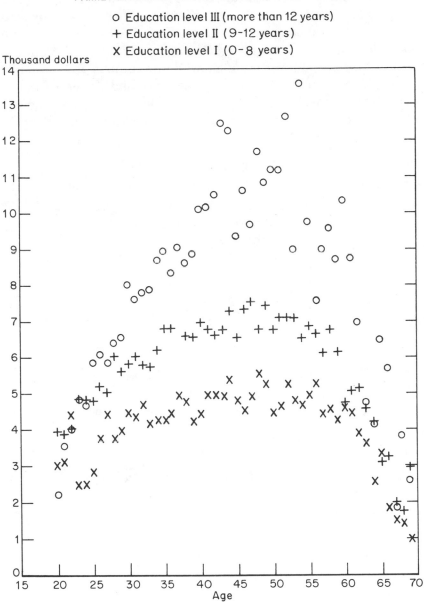

FIGURE 2.2
FAMILY EARNINGS BY AGE AND EDUCATION OF HEAD

O Education level III (more than 12 years)
+ Education level II (9-12 years)
X Education level I (0-8 years)

with more education also rises much more rapidly up to the mid-forties (Figure 2.3). Peak consumption is about two and a half times consumption at early years of age for households in which the head is at least a high school graduate, and less than twice that amount for households with the least-educated heads. This apparent parallel arching of the consumption profiles with the earnings profiles is one of the striking features revealed by the data, and predicted by the theory. Also, as one would expect, the consumption profile of households with more education tends to lie uniformly above that of house-

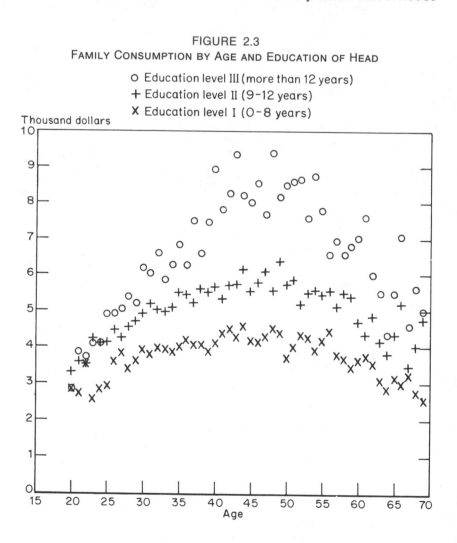

FIGURE 2.3
FAMILY CONSUMPTION BY AGE AND EDUCATION OF HEAD

O Education level III (more than 12 years)
+ Education level II (9-12 years)
X Education level I (0-8 years)

TABLE 2.2
MEAN AND STANDARD DEVIATION OF FAMILY EARNINGS AND CONSUMPTION
BY EDUCATION OF HOUSEHOLD HEAD IN 1960–61

	Earnings		Consumption	
Education Level	Mean	Standard Deviation	Mean	Standard Deviation
All	$6,248	$1,033	$5,149	$ 681
I (0–8 yrs.)	4,496	678	3,925	449
II (9–12 yrs.)	6,231	927	5,222	627
III (13 yrs. or more)	8,755	2,183	6,870	1,440

SOURCE: BLS Survey of Consumer Expenditures, 1960–61. Weighted statistics over age cells ranging from age 22 to 65 (weight = cell size).

holds with less education, because real wealth is greater for those having more schooling. This may be seen also in Table 2.2, which gives means and standard deviations of earnings and consumption by level of schooling.

For all heads combined and within each education group the consumption profile lies below the earnings profile except during old age. Part of the explanation for this is that the services of some durable goods are not included in my measure of consumption. Secondly, each cohort is transferring more assets to future generations than it received from previous ones.

2.5   RESULTS

With observations ordered by age of head, I ran linear regressions of the logarithm of mean consumption of goods on the logarithm of mean earnings, the logarithm of mean family size, and age.[24] The standard format is:

$$\log X_t = B_0 + B_e \log E_t + B_{fs} \log FS_t + B_t t; \qquad (2.10)$$

where

---

24. Similar regressions are presented in Chapter 3 on the life cycle allocation of time. Becker and I recognize that simultaneous equation estimates would have been preferable, but feel strongly that the approach taken here is a useful first step.

X_t = mean family consumption of goods at age t of the head;
E_t = mean family earnings at age t;
FS_t = mean family size at age t.[25]

Regressions are weighted by the square root of cell size in order to reduce heteroscedasticity arising from differences in cell sizes within the sample.[26] Results are presented in Table 2.3 on the lines labeled X.

The coefficients of all the independent variables are positive in all cases. The t values for earnings are high: over 16.0 for all households combined, and ranging from 7.7 to 13.0 within education groups.[27] For family size the t ratio is about 7.8 for the total sample, and ranges from about 3.0 to 6.0 within education groups. For age of head, the t value is 7.0 for the over-all sample and varies from 3.7 to 7.2 in the subsamples.

Estimates obtained using the BLS category "expenditures on current consumption" (ECC) as the dependent variable are also shown in Table 2.3. ECC includes the purchase of all durable goods except dwellings, and underestimates the value of owned housing.[28] It is therefore a hybrid, closer in spirit to a measure of expenditure than to a measure of use of goods. The single most important difference between the ECC series and X stems from the treatment of durable goods. Direct evidence shows that the elasticity of purchases of major durable goods with respect to earnings exceeds the earnings elasticity of demand for many nondurables.[29] The coefficients I obtained for earnings using ECC are positive and slightly larger than those obtained using my constructed measure of consumption (X) (except in the college group). Moreover, the age coefficients are

---

25. On the use of arithmetic means instead of geometric ones, see the appendix to this chapter.

26. For a discussion of weighted regressions when the sample is stratified, see Lawrence Klein, *A Textbook of Econometrics* (Evanston, Ill.: Row, Peterson, 1953).

27. Standard errors have not been adjusted for possible nonindependence of the "time series."

28. For owners of dwellings the BLS survey records interest on mortgages, taxes, and repairs. This is an underestimate of the value of owned housing because mortgage interest is less than total interest forgone, and depreciation is not fully recorded.

29. Using the same basic double log format as in (2.10), I found the coefficient of earnings for all heads combined to be 0.83 for furnishings (net of insurance), 1.22 for automobile purchases, 0.69 for the purchase of durable recreation goods (radio, TV, musical instruments), but only 0.35 for food and 0.29 for adjusted rents. For clothing it is 1.01. All t values exceed 2.

smaller and consistently not significant when *ECC* is the dependent variable. The reason is that *ECC* understates the cost of home ownership, since it includes interest on mortgages, but not on equity. Since equity rises with age, *ECC* understates the cost of home ownership especially at older ages.

A nonzero coefficient for earnings is predicted by the theory developed in Chapter 1. An increase in the price of time raises the demand for goods relative to time and reduces the demand for future goods relative to present ones. The coefficient for the price of time would be zero, sampling and measurement errors aside, only in the

TABLE 2.3

REGRESSIONS FOR CONSUMPTION OF GOODS: ALTERNATIVE MEASURES OF CONSUMPTION

Dependent Variable (in logs)	Inter- cept	Independent Variables (*t* values in parentheses)			Mult. Corr. Coeff.	Adj. R^2	Durbin- Watson
		Log *E*	Log *FS*	Age			
All Education Levels; Ages 22–65							
X	3.4835	0.5253	0.2593	0.0035	.9904	.9794	1.7386
		(16.3577)	(7.7945)	(7.2497)			
ECC	3.4388	0.5580	0.2450	0.0000	.9909	.9804	1.6328
		(16.2703)	(6.8961)	(0.0017)			
Grade School; Ages 22–65							
X	3.6870	0.4859	0.2586	0.0038	.9717	.9401	2.3476
		(13.2405)	(5.9641)	(3.7202)			
ECC	3.7020	0.5105	0.2612	0.0006	.9727	.9422	2.7890
		(12.0483)	(5.2166)	(0.5110)			
High School; Ages 22–65							
X	4.2127	0.4219	0.2932	0.0071	.9577	.9109	2.0118
		(7.7016)	(5.5886)	(7.1918)			
ECC	4.0093	0.4748	0.2789	0.0031	.9592	.9140	2.1920
		(9.0884)	(5.5751)	(3.2708)			
College; Ages 22–65							
X	2.9662	0.6001	0.1746	0.0051	.9659	.9279	2.2035
		(9.8524)	(2.9582)	(3.8379)			
ECC	3.3090	0.5889	0.1592	0.0011	.9620	.9199	2.1413
		(10.4940)	(2.9283)	(0.8740)			

NOTE: *X* = family consumption (see text for items included), *ECC* = BLS concept of expenditures on current consumption, *E* = family earnings, *FS* = family size.

singular case in which substitution in consumption was equal in magnitude to substitution in production. If we interpret family earnings as a measure of the price of time, the positive coefficients for earnings are consistent with the hypothesis that substitution in production is easier than in consumption.[30] The coefficients for earnings are in fact quite large. When all heads are combined it is equal to about 0.53: a 10 per cent rise in family earnings raises the demand for goods by more than 5 per cent.[31]

The test against the null hypothesis that earnings have no effect on consumption over the life cycle is a test against an alternative model of consumption behavior. Under that hypothesis goods provide utility directly, rather than through the production of commodities. Moreover, the allocation of time between work and other activities is determined exogenously, rather than within the model. With a lifetime horizon, perfect capital markets, and no unexpected changes in wealth, the consumption of each household will be the same at all ages if the rate of interest net of time preference is zero and family size is constant. Consumption rises with age if the rate of interest net of time preference is positive or if family size is rising. The rise or fall of consumption will be independent of the rise or fall of earnings. The earnings stream together with interest rates would determine the household's wealth and thus the *level* of the consumption stream, but not the rising or falling of consumption with age. If we assumed that income expectations were unbiased, that model would predict that changes in cohort consumption would be independent of changes in earnings with age. In other words, it predicts that $B_e = 0$ in equation (2.10), sampling and measurement errors

---

30. In the appendix to this chapter, I show that $B_e \gtreqless 0$ as $\sigma_f \gtreqless \sigma_c$. Strictly speaking, the double logarithmic format of equation (2.10) is not completely appropriate when earnings are used as a measure of the price of time, because the elasticity of earnings with respect to the wage rate is not constant.

31. These coefficients are smaller than the usual estimates of the elasticity of consumption with respect to permanent income, but somewhat larger than those of the elasticity of consumption with respect to transitory income. See for instance, Ronald Bodkin, "Windfall Income and Consumption" and Milton Friedman, Comments, in Irving Friend and Robert Jones, eds., *Proceedings of Conference on Consumption and Saving,* vol. 2 (Philadelphia, University of Pennsylvania Press, 1960), pp. 175–187 and 191–212. Also see Jacob Mincer, "Employment and Consumption," *Review of Economics and Statistics* (February 1960), pp. 20–26.

aside. This hypothesis is close in spirit to the Modigliani-Brumberg model of consumption planning,[32] if to their lifetime hypothesis we append the assumption that income expectations are unbiased.

The regressions reported in Table 2.3 provide strong evidence against the simple alternative hypothesis. The coefficient for earnings is well above zero, and the estimates are statistically significant.

Family size exerts a positive effect on consumption. For all heads combined the coefficient of family size is about 0.26: a doubling of family size raises consumption by a little more than 25 per cent. The effect of family size on consumption is in the same direction as the effect of earnings, but it is considerably weaker. A 5 per cent rise in consumption is elicited by a 10 per cent rise in earnings or by a 20 per cent rise in family size over the life cycle.

Family size is included in the regressions to control for some factors which influence the demand for goods (and time).[33] An increase in the number of children per family would raise the demand for the wife's time. To increase her time in the production of child services she would reduce her time spent at work. Eventually, with a sufficiently large family, she would cease working altogether. She would meet any further increase in family size by reducing her time in other, presumably less time-intensive, home activities. Predictions about the effect of changes in family size on goods consumed by the household are not so clear-cut. An increase in the number of children would raise the demand for goods used in child rearing relative to goods used in other nonmarket activities, but it would raise the demand for future goods relatively more than the demand for current ones, as long as older children were more goods-intensive than

---

32. See the references listed in Chapter 1, note 25. See also Franco Modigliani and Albert Ando, "Tests of the Life Cycle Hypothesis of Saving," *Bulletin of the Oxford University Institute of Statistics* (May 1957), p. 105; and Modigliani and Ando, "The Life Cycle Hypothesis of Saving," *American Economic Review* (March 1963), p. 56.

33. A nonzero coefficient for family size is consistent with a wide variety of naive models. If utility depended on goods per unit of family size (or better, per unit of family equivalent), the effect of an increase in family size on goods over the life cycle would be positive or negative according as the elasticity of substitution in consumption was smaller than or greater than unity. Another naive decision rule would be that changes in goods per unit family size depend only on changes in earnings per unit family over the life cycle. This hypothesis is rejected, since the sum of the coefficients for earnings and for family size, $B_e + B_{fs}$, differs significantly from unity.

young ones. In principle, therefore, a control for family age composition as well as size would have been preferable.[34] Moreover, if births and their timing were endogenous, the demand for goods (and time) and the demand for children would be simultaneously determined. A full system to explain all these remains a subject for future research.[35]

The coefficient for age is 0.0035 when all households are combined: in the absence of differences in earnings or in family size, consumption would rise with age in the cross section at a rate of less than one-half of 1 per cent per year of age. Age is a variable often included in regression analyses of consumption behavior. Sometimes the only interpretation offered for the observed effect of age is that tastes may shift with age. More often it is discussed in relation to the changes in income expectations and family size that may occur over the life cycle, and to the importance of credit ceilings.[36] In the context of life cycle behavior, the interpretation of the coefficient of age is clear: it measures the combined effect of interest rates net of time preference and of trends in productivity.

Over all, the basic model seems consistent with the data. The regressions for each level of education are not very different from the over-all regression. Moreover, the R^2 are high, and there is no evidence of serial correlation of the residuals as measured by the Durbin-Watson d statistic.

In order to test the robustness of the findings, I ran the same regressions in first-difference form:

$$\Delta \log X_t = B_e \, \Delta \log E_t + B_{fs} \, \Delta \log FS_t + B_t. \tag{2.11}$$

The estimates are reported on the first line of Table 2.9, below. Again, the coefficients of all the variables are found to be positive and of the

34. See, for instance, Michael Lansberger, "An Integrated Model of Consumption and Market Activity: The Children Effect" (mimeo., 1971). At any rate, instrumental variables estimation techniques would have been more appropriate than ordinary least squares, to account for the simultaneous determination of consumption and family size.

35. For instance, the timing of children is not independent of the timing of marriage.

36. See the rather brief discussions of the effects of age in Milton Friedman, *A Theory of the Consumption Function* (Princeton, N.J.: Princeton University Press for NBER, 1957) and Harold W. Watts, "Long-Run Income Expectations and Consumer Saving," in T. Dernberg et al., eds., *Studies in Household Economic Behavior,* vol. 9 (New Haven: Yale University Press, 1958).

same order of magnitude as in the level equations of (2.10). However, the *t* values are somewhat reduced.

If interest rates or time preference varied systematically with age, or if trends in productivity were not constant, age would not operate linearly on consumption. To test against this alternative, I introduced the square of age into the level regressions of equation (2.10). In Table 2.4, it can be seen that in all samples except that for college-educated heads, the coefficient of age squared is zero.

One effect of the introduction of age squared is to reduce the size of the coefficients for earnings. This suggests that a systematic relation may exist. Mincer has shown that earnings are well explained by years of schooling and a quadratic function of experience.[37] And indeed if years of experience[38] and its square are used, rather than age and its square, to explain consumption, the coefficients for earnings are reduced slightly more (see Table 2.4).

2.6 FURTHER TESTS

In the previous section I showed that earnings exert a positive effect on consumption over the life cycle. This result is consistent with the model of consumption developed in Chapter 1. Yet this does not ensure that the model provides a complete description of behavior. Although I have produced high values of R^2 with a limited set of variables, nevertheless, I may well have neglected some important determinants. Moreover, a positive relationship between consumption and earnings could be predicted under quite different hypotheses. A positive correlation between consumption and earnings is no proof that only substitution effects are at work over the life cycle. Indeed, in general, it may reflect both income and substitution effects and the appropriate task is to determine the relative strength of each. Consider the following model:[39]

$$X_t = b_0 + b_1 P_t + b_2 U_t + \epsilon_t; \tag{2.12}$$

37. See Jacob Mincer, *Schooling, Experience, and Earnings* (New York: NBER, 1974).

38. Years of experience are defined as: Age $- t_s$, where $t_s = 11$ years for the over-all sample, 7 years for the grade school group, 11 years for the high school group, and 15 years for the college group.

39. I am grateful to James Heckman for this formulation.

TABLE 2.4

Regressions for Consumption of Goods: Effects
of Age and Post-school Training
(dependent variable is log of family consumption)

Inter-cept	Independent Variables (*t* values in parentheses)						Mult. Corr. Coeff.	Adj. R^2	Durbin-Watson
	Log E	Log FS	Age	$(Age)^2$	Exp.	$(Exp.)^2$			
All Education Levels; Ages 22–65									
3.5207	0.5189	0.2509	0.0050	−0.0000			.9904	.9789	1.7492
	(10.1785)	(4.1032)	(0.5206)	(−0.1640)					
All Education Levels; Ages 24–65									
3.5682	0.5178	0.2608			0.0046	−0.0000	.9894	.9767	1.7633
	(9.8963)	(3.9859)			(0.6244)	(−0.1265)			
Grade School; Ages 22–65									
3.7148	0.4809	0.2486	0.0053	−0.0000			.9718	.9386	2.3277
	(10.8285)	(3.7892)	(0.7200)	(−0.2053)					
Grade School; Ages 20–65									
3.7503	0.4796	0.2525			0.0052	−0.0000	.9724	.9403	2.3474
	(11.0454)	(3.9897)			(0.8790)	(−0.2226)			
High School; Ages 22–65									
4.3760	0.3958	0.2583	0.0130	−0.0001			.9578	.9090	2.0478
	(4.6103)	(2.5227)	(0.8749)	(−0.3990)					
High School; Ages 24–65									
4.6027	0.3786	0.2769			0.0131	−0.0001	.9502	.8924	2.0678
	(4.2835)	(2.5051)			(1.1742)	(−0.4817)			
College; Ages 22–65									
3.3282	0.4721	−0.0404	0.0588	−0.0006			.9708	.9365	2.0963
	(6.1930)	(−0.3992)	(2.7734)	(−2.5389)					
College; Ages 28–65									
3.9957	0.4699	0.0159			0.0389	−0.0006	.9460	.8822	2.2341
	(5.6297)	(0.1282)			(2.5920)	(−2.1849)			

Note: E = family earnings, FS = family size, Exp. = experience in the labor market.

where

P_t = life cycle or permanent level of earnings appropriate to age group t;

U_t = deviation of measured earnings from their life cycle component, i.e., $E = P + U$;

ϵ_t = disturbance term.

The relation as written in equation (2.10) is misspecified. To examine the bias, write equation (2.12) as

$$X_t = b_0 + b_1 E_t + (b_2 - b_1)U_t + \epsilon_t. \tag{2.13}$$

The bias in the estimate of b_1 from the omission of the "measurement error" U_t is $E(\hat{b}_1) - b_1 = (b_2 - b_1)b_{eu}$, where $E(\hat{b}_1)$ is the expected value of the least squares estimate of b_1, and b_{eu} is the regression coefficient in a regression of the omitted variable U on the included variable E; in other words,

$$b_{eu} = \frac{\text{covariance }(E_t, U_t)}{\text{variance }(E_t)}.$$

If we assume there to be no correlation in the sample between permanent levels P_t and "measurement error" U_t, then [40]

$$b_{eu} = \frac{\text{variance }(U_t)}{\text{variance }(P_t) + \text{variance }(U_t)}.$$

If we approximate the numerator by the sampling variance of the mean for a typical age group, an estimate of b_{eu} can be obtained. Table 2.5 contains values of the variance of family earnings by selected years of age of the household head. This variance essentially rises with age and years of schooling. Using the variance at age 40 (which is close to the mean age in the sample), and the variance of mean earnings across age groups we get the estimates of b_{eu} in Table 2.6. On the face of it, the bias resulting from income effects is relatively small.

Regressions reported in Table 2.3 explained variations in consumption by variations in earnings, family size, and age. In order to treat the components of income more symmetrically, I introduce non-wage income, R, as an additional variable. It is computed as the dif-

---

40. In equation (2.12) and therefore in the expression for b_{eu}, all variables are in logarithms. The calculations of b_{eu} below take account of this fact.

TABLE 2.5
VARIANCE OF FAMILY EARNINGS BY SELECTED YEARS OF AGE
AND EDUCATION LEVEL OF THE HOUSEHOLD HEAD, 1960–61
(millions of dollars)

Age of Household Head	Education Level			
	All	I	II	III
25	5.93	2.51	4.30	7.34
30	13.92	7.07	9.28	18.88
35	15.10	6.98	12.26	17.78
40	18.76	10.42	12.23	23.60
45	16.16	7.44	13.65	26.65
50	24.37	10.16	16.11	39.46
55	18.70	12.97	14.37	24.06
60	27.71	13.54	16.90	64.66
65	22.78	18.36	10.40	58.73

SOURCE: BLS Survey of Consumer Expenditures, 1960–61.

TABLE 2.6
COMPUTATION OF REGRESSION BIAS

	Education Level			
	All	I	II	III
1. Estimate of the variance of the log of earnings at age 40 [a]	0.37	0.53	0.25	0.23
2. Cell size at age 40	337	88	169	80
3. Variance of the log of mean earnings across age groups	0.04	0.03	0.03	0.02
b_{eu}	0.03	0.17	0.05	0.10

NOTE: $b_{eu} = $ (line 1/line 2)/[line 3 + (line 1/line 2)].
SOURCE: BLS Survey of Consumer Expenditures, 1960–61.
a. This estimate is a linear approximation (around mean earnings at age 40) to the variance of the logarithm of earnings at age 40: it is equal to the square of the coefficient of variation of earnings at age 40. For this computation, I used the variances given in Table 2.5.

ference between total family income, Y, and family earnings, E, and is entered in the regression in logarithmic form. Results are given in Table 2.8, below (first line). Nonwage income exerts a positive effect on consumption over the life cycle. The t ratio is 3.8 when all households are combined, and ranges from 1.9 to 2.9 within education classes. In all cases the size of the coefficient is relatively small. It is about 0.066 for all households combined and is of the same order of magnitude within each education group: a 10 per cent rise in nonwage income raises family consumption by approximately two-thirds of 1 per cent.

If cohort expectations about nonwage income were unbiased, savings would be undertaken simply to make the consumption program feasible. After some initial period of indebtedness, assets would rise, reaching a peak well beyond the peak earnings age, and then contract as the household retires. The general life cycle path of assets is given in Table 2.7, as it appeared in a 1962 survey. The decline in assets sets in after age 65.

Nonwage income can be computed with the BLS data as the difference between income and earnings. One component is the yield on transferable assets; with a fixed rate of interest this component would be proportional to assets themselves. Other components are alimony, social security, and pension payments, much of which comes

TABLE 2.7
MEAN NET WORTH OF CONSUMER UNITS
BY AGE OF HEAD, DECEMBER 31, 1962

Age of Head	Mean Net Worth
Under 25	$ 557
25–34	4,831
35–44	14,792
45–54	22,237
55–64	32,511
65 and over	30,124

SOURCE: Dorothy S. Projector, *Survey of Changes in Family Finances* (Board of Governors of the Federal Reserve System, 1968), Table S 17.

late in life. The over-all pattern of nonwage income in the BLS survey, as in other surveys,[41] is that it rises primarily with age.

If expectations about nonwage income were continuously fulfilled, the theory predicts that nonwage income would have no effect on consumption over the life cycle, sampling and measurement errors aside. A positive effect of nonwage income on consumption over the life cycle could be interpreted as resulting from incorrect expectations about nonwage income.

The coefficients for nonwage income in Table 2.8 (first line) are positive, but about one-tenth the size of those for earnings.[42] The modest size of the coefficients is consistent with the emphasis of my model on the greater importance of variations in earnings compared to variations in nonwage income in explaining life cycle consumption, which is based on the observation that the former give rise to substitution effects, while the latter do not. The positive signs of the coefficients of nonwage income lend some credibility to the notion that future income is not perfectly predicted. It is also noteworthy that the coefficients of age and the t values are reduced when nonwage income is included in the regression, owing to the positive correlation of the latter with age.

Another, quite different, interpretation of the positive coefficient for nonwage income is that households cannot borrow and lend at fixed rates of interest, but that the cost of transferring income over time largely depends on the household's net indebtedness.[43] An extreme version of credit rationing is one in which consumption is entirely constrained by current income. In order to test against this hypothesis, I calculated the regression of consumption on total income, nonwage income, family size, and age (all variables in logs except age). Results are presented in Table 2.8 (second line for each category). Total income has a positive effect on consumption: the coefficient is about 0.72 when all households are combined, and

41. This is true for instance in the 1/1,000 sample of U.S. population, 1960, and in the Survey of Economic Opportunity, 1967.

42. Becker also finds positive coefficients for other income in his regressions for male time, but his are smaller in magnitude (see Table 3.1, below). Barring measurement errors, these coefficients should be of the same size given constant returns to scale in production.

43. A discussion of this hypothesis is given in Gilbert R. Ghez, "Life Cycle Consumption in the Presence of Segmentation in the Capital Market" (unpublished, 1968).

TABLE 2.8
REGRESSIONS FOR CONSUMPTION OF GOODS: EFFECTS OF NONWAGE INCOME
(dependent variable is log of family consumption)

| Inter-cept | Independent Variables (*t* values in parentheses) | | | | | Mult. Corr. Coeff. | Adj. R² | Durbin-Watson |
	Log E	Log R	Log Y	Log FS	Age			
	**All Education Levels; Ages 22–65**							
2.0967	0.5528	0.0656		0.2489	0.0018	.9930	.9845	2.0443
	(19.2407)	(3.7914)		(8.6043)	(3.0834)			
1.9663		−0.0027	0.7157	0.1916	0.0008	.9924	.9833	1.9414
		(−0.1570)	(18.4428)	(5.8391)	(1.2199)			
	**All Education Levels; Ages 35–65**							
2.7970	0.5267	0.0626		0.3886	0.0057	.9948	.9881	2.7354
	(17.1997)	(2.9391)		(6.8324)	(3.6753)			
2.0228		−0.0145	0.6753	0.3377	0.0049	.9945	.9873	2.6631
		(−0.7122)	(16.5907)	(5.5320)	(3.0286)			
	**Grade School; Ages 22–65**							
3.2739	0.5106	0.0455		0.2458	0.0025	.9745	.9444	2.3735
	(13.6623)	(2.0314)		(5.8192)	(2.1385)			
2.5882		−0.0130	0.6310	0.2373	0.0020	.9759	.9474	2.2835
		(−0.6225)	(14.1268)	(5.7356)	(1.7157)			
	**Grade School; Ages 35–65**							
3.2612	0.4945	0.0553		0.2846	0.0033	.9732	.9389	2.4465
	(10.5647)	(1.7835)		(3.5241)	(1.2827)			
2.5977		−0.0147	0.6218	0.2666	0.0029	.9741	.9409	2.3364
		(−0.4982)	(10.7868)	(3.3244)	(1.1377)			
	**High School; Ages 22–65**							
3.3693	0.4812	0.0677		0.2847	0.0050	.9637	.9215	1.8205
	(8.5113)	(2.5258)		(5.7658)	(3.9916)			
2.0412		0.0049	0.6921	0.2095	0.0029	.9692	.9331	1.7918
		(0.2152)	(9.5792)	(4.1441)	(2.2005)			
	**High School; Ages 35–65**							
2.3956	0.5370	0.1057		0.3857	0.0075	.9346	.8539	1.8002
	(7.7549)	(3.0787)		(3.9677)	(2.6665)			
0.5297		0.0423	0.8103	0.3038	0.0051	.9555	.8996	1.8375
		(1.7134)	(9.9672)	(3.6588)	(2.1443)			
	**College; Ages 22–65**							
2.6320	0.6068	0.0542		0.1680	0.0031	.9706	.9362	2.3635
	(10.5800)	(2.4925)		(3.0228)	(2.1120)			
2.1255		−0.0119	0.7087	0.1599	0.0022	.9666	.9277	2.2982
		(−0.4985)	(9.7013)	(2.6344)	(1.3385)			
	**College; Ages 35–65**							
2.9065	0.6013	0.0521		0.1034	0.0005	.9127	.8074	2.2430
	(8.9805)	(1.4604)		(0.7962)	(0.1044)			
2.3753		−0.0355	0.7146	0.1117	0.0006	.9037	.7884	2.2579
		(−0.9243)	(8.4318)	(0.8207)	(0.1319)			

NOTE: E = family earnings, R = family nonwage income, Y = family income, FS = family size.

ranges from 0.63 to 0.71 within education classes; all these coefficients have high *t* values. Nonwage income has a very slight, usually negative, effect on consumption (when holding total income constant), but none of the estimates is statistically different from zero. The same results appear in the first-difference regressions given in Table 2.9.

TABLE 2.9

REGRESSIONS FOR CONSUMPTION OF GOODS: FIRST-DIFFERENCE EQUATIONS
(dependent variable is Δ log family consumption)

Inter-cept	Independent Variables (t values in parentheses)				Mult. Corr. Coeff.	Adj. R²	Durbin-Watson
	Δ Log E	Δ Log R	Δ Log Y	Δ Log FS			
All Education Levels; Ages 22–65							
.0045	0.5377 (9.4550)			0.2675 (3.1582)	.8882	.7783	3.0556
.0028	0.5608 (10.4666)	0.0507 (2.6925)		0.2698 (3.4253)	.9066	.8083	3.0747
.0011		−0.0061 (−0.3261)	0.6423 (0.4250)	0.2515 (3.1539)	.9061	.8072	3.0631
Grade School; Ages 22–65							
.0026	0.4642 (8.6485)			0.1815 (2.3061)	.8406	.6919	2.8512
.0003	0.4769 (9.1396)	0.0454 (1.9908)		0.1759 (2.3138)	.8565	.7131	2.7757
−.0010		−0.0011 (−0.0495)	0.5685 (10.0180)	0.1687 (2.3653)	.8751	.7478	2.7063
High School; Ages 22–65							
.0098	0.4041 (4.2662)			0.3464 (2.7413)	.6771	.4314	2.5312
.0072	0.4076 (4.9316)	0.0889 (3.6782)		0.3946 (3.5533)	.7732	.5670	2.4095
.0044		0.0343 (1.4495)	0.5794 (6.1248)	0.3290 (3.1861)	.8169	.6417	2.4700
College; Ages 22–65							
.0074	0.5495 (6.7195)			−0.1262 (−1.1860)	.7308	.5108	2.9477
.0057	0.5739 (7.1951)	0.0433 (2.0113)		−0.1353 (−1.3178)	.7602	.5454	2.9197
.0052		−0.0210 (−0.8846)	0.6477 (6.2977)	−0.1172 (−1.0639)	.7162	.4754	2.9722

NOTE: Δ = first-difference operator taken over adjacent years of age, E = family earnings, R = family nonwage income, Y = family income, FS = family size.

According to the theory developed in Chapter 1, variations in consumption do not depend on variations in nonwage income over the life cycle. The coefficient for total income measures the effect of changes in earnings on changes in consumption. On the other hand, with total income held constant a rise in nonwage income must be accompanied by a fall in earnings. Hence the model in Chapter 1 would predict that with total income held constant the coefficient for nonwage income should have a sign opposite to that of total income. Moreover, since the regressions are logarithmic, the coefficient for nonwage income should equal in absolute value the product of the elasticity of consumption with respect to earnings multiplied by the ratio of nonwage income to earnings. In other words, the absolute value of the ratio of the coefficient for nonwage income to that of total income should equal the ratio of nonwage income to total income. While the prediction on the relative signs of the coefficients is borne out in the regressions, the prediction about their relative magnitude is not, since nonwage income accounts for about 25 per cent of total income.[44]

The absolute income hypothesis seems to explain this body of data remarkably well. It is well known, however, that this hypothesis has been rejected on many grounds and with much evidence.[45] In particular, it fails to reconcile the secular stability of the savings ratio with the declining average propensity to consume observed in cross sections.

One possible interpretation is that nonwage income is poorly measured. This would bias the coefficient of nonwage income downward and that of total income upward.[46] Another interpretation is that if credit rationing exists, it must surely operate more severely for borrowers than for lenders. It might be expected that if the years of age in which households are heavy borrowers are excluded, the pre-

---

44. This method of testing is by no means accurate, since the expected value of the ratio of two parameter estimates is not equal to the ratio of the expected values of these estimates. Approximate tests would have been more appropriate.

45. To name but a few pieces in this voluminous literature, see Friedman, *Theory of the Consumption Function;* Hendrik H. Houthakker, "The Permanent Income Hypothesis," *American Economic Review* (June 1958); Robert Eisner, Comment, *American Economic Review* (December 1958); Michael K. Evans, "The Importance of Wealth in the Consumption Function," *Journal of Political Economy* (August 1967), pp. 335–351.

46. One may also suggest that the BLS in its attempt to reconcile expenditures and incomes introduces a systematic positive association between consumption and income.

dictions of the theory developed in Chapter 1 would be more clearly borne out. For this purpose, I ran regressions similar to those in Table 2.8 (second line) but including only households in which the head was at least 35 years old. The results are also given in Table 2.8. They are somewhat better than the results obtained with the wider sample: the coefficients for nonwage income, still negative, are slightly increased in absolute value, both for all households combined and within education groups. Moreover, the significance levels of these estimates is slightly increased (except in the case of high school heads).

2.7   SUMMARY

In this chapter, an attempt was made to provide orders of magnitude of the responsiveness of the consumption of goods to its determinants over the life cycle. Using the Bureau of Labor Statistics Survey of Consumer Expenditures for 1960–61, the following main conclusions were drawn:

i. Consumption responds positively to earnings over the life cycle. A 10 per cent rise in earnings raises consumption by about 5 per cent.

ii. This positive response can result from three main sources: (a) substitution effects as described in Chapter 1, (b) income effects resulting from incorrect income and wage rate expectations, and (c) income effects resulting from credit rationing. While income effects are present in the estimates, they by no means account fully for the positive response of consumption to earnings. In other words, the substitution effects resulting from lifetime changes in the wage rate do play a role in determining life cycle consumption.

iii. Increases in family size tend to raise consumption, a finding consistent with that of many other studies.

iv. The consumption profile has a positive trend in the cross section. Put differently, age of head has an independent effect on consumption. This effect is the combined result of interest rate plus time preference effects and time series trends in productivity that are captured by drawing observations from different cohorts in a cross section.

v. In sum, from a relatively complicated model a rather simple estimating equation was developed. Results obtained when the equation was applied to observed cross-cohort consumption behavior are essentially consistent with the theory. Other interpretations are possible, but many of these lack a theoretical basis. The general theoretical framework, which stresses the importance of time in the home, is capable of generating many other hypotheses which also appear to be supported by existing evidence (see the references given in the Introduction to this volume). It is the wide applicability and broad explanatory power of the framework that is encouraging evidence of its usefulness. In Chapter 3 Becker provides yet another piece of evidence related to the life cycle model — the allocation of hours worked by men over their lifetime. In Chapter 4, the estimates obtained are used to interpret still other bodies of data.

APPENDIX

In this appendix, I examine the possible biases arising from (1) nonconstant factor shares, (2) the use of arithmetic means rather than geometric ones, (3) the use of earnings rather than wage rates as the price of time.

For simplicity of presentation, I assume that the family is composed of only one earner. I assume also that elasticities of substitution in consumption and in production are constant, and that technological change in the household is factor-neutral.

1   ON THE CONSTANCY OF FACTOR SHARES

For any given individual the change in demand for goods and time at age t are [47]

$$\tilde{X}_t = \hat{W}_t - (1 - \sigma_c)\hat{P}_t + (\sigma_f - \sigma_c)s\bar{w}_t - (1 - \sigma_c)\tilde{F}_t + \sigma_c(r - \rho); \quad \text{(A2.1)}$$

$$\tilde{L}_t = \hat{W}_t - (1 - \sigma_c)\hat{P}_t - [\sigma_f(1 - s) + \sigma_c s]\bar{w}_t - (1 - \sigma_c)\tilde{F}_t + \sigma_c(r - \rho); \quad \text{(A2.2)}$$

where s is the share of time in the cost of commodities, and other variables are defined in the text. With factor-neutral technological changes in the household, the share s would rise, fall, or remain the same as the wage rate rose, depending on whether the elasticity of substitution in production was smaller than, greater than, or equal to unity. Suppose we approximated

---

47. All prices and incomes are in terms of goods. Asterisks were used in the text to distinguish them, but are omitted here to simplify the notation.

the share of time by [48]

$$s_t = \Phi_1 + \Phi_2 \log w_t, \tag{A2.3}$$

with $\Phi_2 \gtreqless 0$ as $\sigma_f \lesseqgtr 1$. The change in the price of commodities arising from a percentage change in the wage rate, $\tilde{w}$, is $s\tilde{w}$. Since

$$s_t \tilde{w}_t \cong s_t \frac{d \log w_t}{dt} = \Phi_1 \left(\frac{d \log w}{dt} \right) + \Phi_2 \log w \left(\frac{d \log w}{dt} \right), \tag{A2.4}$$

its integral is

$$\Phi_1(\log w_t) + \frac{\Phi_2}{2} (\log w_t)^2 + \Phi_0. \tag{A2.5}$$

Let $\bar{x}$ denote the geometric mean of the variable x. If we obtain the regression of the mean of consumption by age on age and on the mean wage rate by age, as in $\log \bar{X}_t = b_0 + b_w \log \bar{\bar{w}}_t + b_t t$, we would be omitting the quadratic term

$$\frac{1}{n_t} \sum_{i=1}^{n_t} (\log w_t)^2 \equiv Q_t,$$

where the summation runs over the n_t individuals of age t.[49] The bias in the estimate of b_w would be equal to the product of $\Phi_2/2$ and the regression coefficient of the linear term $\log \bar{\bar{w}}$ in a regression of Q_t on $\log \bar{\bar{w}}_t$ and t. Since this regression coefficient is bound to be positive and

$$\Phi_2 \gtreqless 0 \text{ as } \sigma_f \lesseqgtr 1,$$

---

48. This is a first-order approximation to the share given by the production function with constant elasticity of substitution. Indeed, when

$$C = (\delta_1 L^{(\sigma-1)/\sigma} + \delta_x X^{(\sigma-1)/\sigma})^{\sigma/(\sigma-1)},$$

with $\delta_1 + \delta_x = 1$, the share of time is

$$s = \frac{\delta_1^\sigma w^{1-\sigma}}{d_1^\sigma w^{1-\sigma} + \delta_x}.$$

A Taylor expansion of s around $\sigma = 1$, dropping second- and higher-order terms, is

$$s = \delta_1 + \delta_1(\log \delta_1 - \delta_1 \log \delta_1 - \delta_x \log \delta_x)(\sigma - 1) - \delta_1(1 - \delta_1)(\log w)(\sigma - 1),$$

or $s = \Phi_1 + \Phi_2 \log w$, with

$$\Phi_1 = \delta_1 + \delta_1(\sigma - 1)(\log \delta_1 - \delta_1 \log \delta_1 - \delta_x \log \delta_x);$$

$$\Phi_2 = \delta_1(1 - \delta_1)(1 - \sigma),$$

so that Φ_1 tends to δ_a and Φ_2 tends to zero as σ tends to unity.

49. There is no bias from omission of a wealth variable, given the expectation model developed in section 2.2. Moreover, there is no bias from omission of a variable for nonmarket productivity, since technological change in the household sector is assumed to be disembodied.

the least squares estimate of b_w would be biased upward, downward, or not biased according as σ_f is less than, more than, or equal to 1.

2 On the Use of Arithmetic Means

Suppose that factor shares were constant. We would then have the exact expressions appropriate for the cross section:

$$\log \bar{\bar{X}}_t = b_0 + b_w \log \bar{\bar{w}}_t + b_t t; \tag{A2.6}$$

$$\log \bar{\bar{L}}_t = a_0 + a_w \log \bar{\bar{w}}_t + a_t t; \tag{A2.7}$$

with

$$b_w = (\sigma_f - \sigma_c)s;$$

$$a_w = -[\sigma_c s + \sigma_f(1 - s)];$$

$$b_t = a_t = \sigma_c(r - \rho) - [1 - s + \sigma_c s]g_w - (1 - \sigma_c)g_f.$$

I shall suppose that the elasticities b_w, a_w, b_t, and a_t are unchanged if we use arithmetic means rather than geometric ones; the only effect of the change of variable is to change the value of the intercept. We can then in principle write (leaving out the disturbance terms):

$$\log \bar{X}_t = b_0' + b_w \log \bar{w}_t + b_t t; \tag{A2.8}$$

$$\log \bar{L}_t = a_0' + a_w \log \bar{w}_t + a_t t; \tag{A2.9}$$

where $\bar{x}$ is the arithmetic mean of the variable x. The validity of this substitution has been given elsewhere.[50] In brief, if any variable x is log-normally distributed, then the difference between its mean logarithm and the logarithm of its mean is equal to (minus) one-half the variance of its logarithm:

$$\log \bar{\bar{x}} \equiv \frac{1}{n} \Sigma \log x = \log \bar{x} - \frac{1}{2} \text{var} (\log x), \tag{A2.10}$$

where $\bar{x}$ is the arithmetic mean and var denotes variance. Therefore, on the assumption that at any given year of age wage rates, real wealth, and goods are log-normally distributed, and that the variances of the logarithms of these variables are constant, the intercept b_0' would also be constant, and would be related to b_0 in the following way:

$$b_0' = b_0 + \frac{1}{2} \text{var} (\log X; t) - \frac{1}{2} b_w \text{var} (\log w; t). \tag{A2.11}$$

If consumption time were also log-normally distributed, the intercept a_0' would be constant and related to a_0 as follows:

$$a_0' = a_0 + \frac{1}{2} \text{var} (\log L; t) - \frac{1}{2} a_w \text{var} (\log w; t). \tag{A2.12}$$

---

50. See J. Aitchison and J. A. C. Brown, *The Lognormal Distribution* (Cambridge, Engl.: Cambridge University Press, 1963).

3   ON THE USE OF EARNINGS AS THE PRICE OF TIME

I now show how the coefficients are affected if earnings rather than wages are used as a measure of the price of time.

By definition earnings per period, E, are the product of wage rates and hours of work, N. If no investment in human capital were made at a given age and if no other time were "lost," hours of work at that age would be the mere image of hours spent in consumption:

$$E_t = w_t N_t = w_t(\theta - L_t). \tag{A2.13}$$

From the definition of a covariance, mean earnings at age t, $\bar{E}_t$, are

$$\bar{E}_t = \text{cov}\,(w_t,\, N_t;\, t) + \bar{w}_t \bar{N}_t; \tag{A2.14}$$

where cov $(w, N; t)$ is the covariance between wage rates and hours of work at age t. I shall suppose that this covariance is the same at all ages. The cross-sectional difference between mean earnings of households at age $t+1$ of the head and at age t is then

$$\bar{E}_{t+1} - \bar{E}_t = \bar{w}_t(\bar{N}_{t+1} - \bar{N}_t) + \bar{N}_t(\bar{w}_{t+1} - \bar{w}_t);$$

and the percentage difference in mean earnings by age is

$$\dot{E}_t = \left(\frac{\bar{w}_t \bar{N}_t}{\bar{E}_t}\right) \dot{N}_t + \left(\frac{\bar{w}_t \bar{N}_t}{\bar{E}_t}\right) \dot{w}_t; \tag{A2.15}$$

where $\dot{x}_t = (\bar{x}_{t+1} - \bar{x}_t)/\bar{x}_t$ in the cross section. But since $N = \theta - L$, we can relate differences in earnings to differences in wage rates by substituting equation (A2.9) into equation (A2.15):

$$\dot{E}_t = -\frac{\bar{w}_t \bar{L}_t}{\bar{E}_t} \dot{L}_t + \frac{\bar{w}_t \bar{N}_t}{\bar{E}_t} \dot{w}_t$$

$$= -\frac{\bar{w}_t \bar{L}_t}{\bar{E}_t} [a_w \dot{w} + a_t] + \frac{\bar{w}_t \bar{N}_t}{\bar{E}_t} \dot{w}_t$$

$$= c_w \dot{w}_t + c_t a_t; \tag{A2.16}$$

where $c_w = (\bar{w}_t \bar{N}_t - \bar{w}_t \bar{L}_t a_w)/\bar{E}_t$ and $c_t = -\bar{w}_t \bar{L}_t/\bar{E}_t$. The elasticity c_w is necessarily positive since $a_w < 0$ over the life cycle, according to the theory developed in Chapter 1. Changes in earnings are positively related to changes in wage rates, because changes in hours of work are positively related to changes in wage rates. The elasticity c_t is negative: hours of work and therefore earnings peak sooner than wage rates if interest rates net of time preference and growth effects are positive.

Notice also that if, at any given age, the covariance between wage rates and hours of work is small, hence $\bar{E}_t \cong \bar{w}_t \bar{N}_t$, then the elasticity $c_w \cong 1 - (\bar{L}_t/\bar{N}_t)a_w$ and the elasticity $c_t \cong - (\bar{L}_t/\bar{N}_t)$. Therefore if cov $(w, N; t) = 0$, c_w is necessarily greater than unity. More generally

$$c_w = 1 - \frac{\bar{w}_t \bar{L}_t a_w}{\bar{E}_t} - \frac{\text{cov } (w, N; t)}{\bar{E}_t};$$

hence $c_w > 1$ unless the covariance between wages and hours of work at any given age is sufficiently positive. As long as differences in wage rates are accompanied by differences in real wealth among households and under the usual assumption that wealth effects dominate substitution effects on the supply of labor, we expect the covariance between wages and hours of work at any given age to be negative, and therefore,

$$c_w > 1 - \frac{\bar{w}_t \bar{L}_t}{\bar{E}_t} a_w > 1. \tag{A2.17}$$

Now suppose that instead of taking regressions of changes in mean consumption of goods on changes in the price of time measured by mean wage rates, as in (A2.8), $\dot{X}_t = b_w \dot{w}_t + b_t$, I used earnings as a measure of the price of time:

$$\dot{X}_t = B_e \dot{\bar{E}}_t + B_t, \tag{A2.18}$$

with

$$B_e = b_w / c_w, \tag{A2.19}$$

where c_w, defined in (A2.16), measures the effect on earnings of changes in wage rates. Since $c_w > 0$, and since $b_w = (\sigma_f - \sigma_c)s$ with $s > 0$, we have

$$B_e \gtreqless 0 \text{ as } \sigma_f \gtreqless \sigma_c. \tag{A2.20}$$

Under the plausible assumption that $c_w > 1$,

$$|B_e| < |b_w|. \tag{A2.21}$$

On the other hand, the relation between B_t, the effect on consumption of interest rates net of time preference and growth when earnings are used to measure the price of time, and b_t, the effect of these parameters when wage rates are used, is given by $b_t = B_t + B_e c_t a_t$, or

$$B_t = b_t(1 - B_e c_t), \tag{A2.22}$$

since $a_t = b_t$. Since c_t, the effect of trends on earnings is negative, $|B_t/b_t| \gtreqless 1$ as $B_e \gtreqless 0$, or using (A2.19):

$$|B_t / b_t| \gtreqless 1 \text{ as } \sigma_f \gtreqless \sigma_c. \tag{A2.23}$$

The interpretation is clear: since earnings peak sooner than wage rates, wage rates will still be rising when earnings reach a peak. Hence, when earnings are at a peak, the consumption of goods will be rising or falling as σ_f is greater than or less than σ_c.

Now consider the ratio of B_t to B_e:

$$\frac{B_t}{B_e} = \frac{b_t}{b_w} (c_w - c_t b_w)$$

$$= \frac{b_t}{b_w} \left[\frac{\bar{w}_t \bar{L}_t}{\bar{E}_t} (b_w - a_w) + \frac{\bar{w}_t \bar{N}_t}{\bar{E}_t} \right]; \tag{A2.24}$$

with c_w and c_t defined as in (A2.16). But

$$b_w - a_w = \sigma_f. \tag{A2.25}$$

Therefore,

$$\frac{B_t}{B_e} = \frac{b_t}{b_w} \left(\frac{\bar{w}_t \bar{L}_t}{\bar{E}_t} \sigma_f + \frac{\bar{w}_t \bar{N}_t}{\bar{E}_t} \right)$$

or

$$\frac{B_t}{B_e} = \frac{b_t}{b_w} \left[\frac{\bar{w}_t \bar{L}_t}{\bar{E}_t} (\sigma_f - 1) + \frac{\bar{w}_t \theta}{\bar{E}_t} \right]. \tag{A2.26}$$

In particular, if $\sigma_f = 1$,

$$\frac{B_t}{B_e} = \frac{b_t}{b_w} \frac{\bar{w}_t \theta}{\bar{E}_t}.$$

Since $\bar{w}_t \theta > \bar{E}_t$, we have

$$\frac{B_t}{B_e} > \frac{b_t}{b_w}. \tag{A2.27}$$

The extension of these results to the case where both husband and wife are earners is straightforward. If for instance the wife's wage rate is approximately constant over time, the conditions (A2.20), (A2.21), (A2.23), and (A2.27) would still apply, with b_w now interpreted to be the coefficient of the wage of the husband.

3

The Allocation of Time
Over the Life Cycle

In this chapter the allocation of time by men over their lifetime is analyzed. As in Ghez's study of consumption in Chapter 2, information on different cohorts at a given time is used because information on a single cohort at different ages is lacking. The main source of information is the 1960 Census, in particular, the 1/1,000 sample. For each of the over 180,000 persons in this sample, information is given about the respondent's sex, race, weeks worked in 1959, hours worked in the census week of 1960, earnings and other income in 1959, years of schooling completed as of 1960, the family size in 1960, and family income in 1959. For the empirical work in this chapter a subsample of some 34,000 employed men has been used. The appendix to this chapter contains more detailed information on the nature of the subsample. Total hours worked in 1959 of each person in this subsample are estimated as the product of his weeks worked in 1959 and his hours worked in the census week. Weekly and hourly wage rates in 1959 are estimated respectively as the ratio of his annual earnings to his weeks worked and to my estimate of his hours worked in 1959. Errors in the estimates of weeks and hours

NOTE: Becker is solely responsible for this chapter.

worked cause errors in the opposite direction in these estimates of weekly and hourly earnings. The different variables were averaged arithmetically for all men of the same age, race, and years of schooling.

Five-year moving averages of average annual hours worked and average hourly earnings are plotted in Figures 3.1 to 3.8, separately for white and nonwhite men of different ages and four schooling classes. Consistent with the substantial evidence on age-earnings profiles, these age and wage rate profiles rise relatively rapidly up to about age 40 and later taper off. One surprise, however, is that wage rate profiles, unlike earnings profiles, do not really fall before age 65 for whites. Either they reach a plateau (see Figure 3.1 for all male whites) or they continue to rise (see Figure 3.4 for male whites with 13 years or more of schooling).

Annual hours worked also rise quite rapidly at young ages and then more slowly. Instead of continuing to rise, however, they peak at a relatively early age, generally in the late thirties, and then decline gradually. This explains why earning profiles, unlike wage rate profiles, generally do peak and begin to decline before age 65. Clearly almost all the evidence in the figures confirms the prediction of the theory in Chapter 1 that hours of work reach a peak (hours of consumption reach a trough) earlier than wage rates.

A finding of some studies is that young persons not enrolled in school have much "unexplained" time; that is, time when they are not employed, looking for work, in training, or sick.[1] They may be traveling, plotting the revolution, or most commonly simply "hanging around." The importance of "unexplained" time is consistent with the evidence in the figures of relatively few hours worked at young ages. Both the "unexplained" time and the relatively few hours worked are explained in our theory by the incentive to use time in nonmarket activities when wage rates are low; that is, to use relatively time-intensive methods of producing consumption commodities. This allocation away from work and toward consumption at young ages makes it difficult to estimate the earnings forgone of those persons who remain in school.[2]

---

1. See *School and Early Employment Experience of Youth: A Report on Seven Communities, 1952–57,* BLS Bull. 1277, 1960, especially Table 20.

2. See the discussion of this problem in Gary S. Becker, *Human Capital,* 1st ed. (New York: NBER, 1964), pp. 169–172.

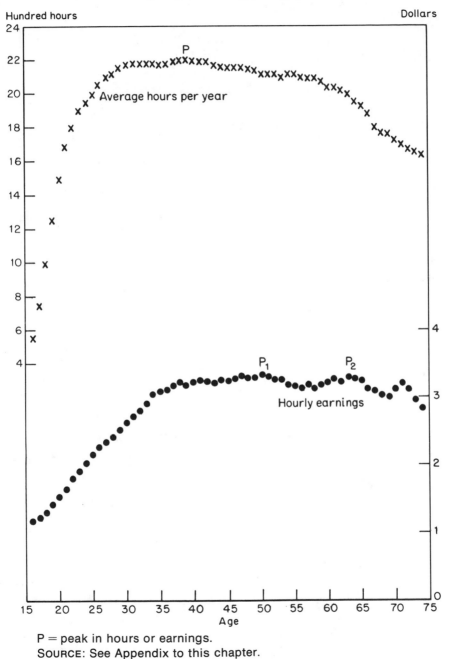

FIGURE 3.1

HOURLY EARNINGS AND AVERAGE HOURS PER YEAR, TOTAL UNITED STATES, ALL EMPLOYED WHITE MEN, ALL EDUCATION LEVELS COMBINED
(five-year moving average)

P = peak in hours or earnings.
SOURCE: See Appendix to this chapter.

85

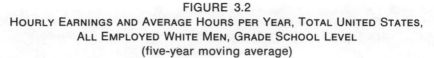

FIGURE 3.2
HOURLY EARNINGS AND AVERAGE HOURS PER YEAR, TOTAL UNITED STATES,
ALL EMPLOYED WHITE MEN, GRADE SCHOOL LEVEL
(five-year moving average)

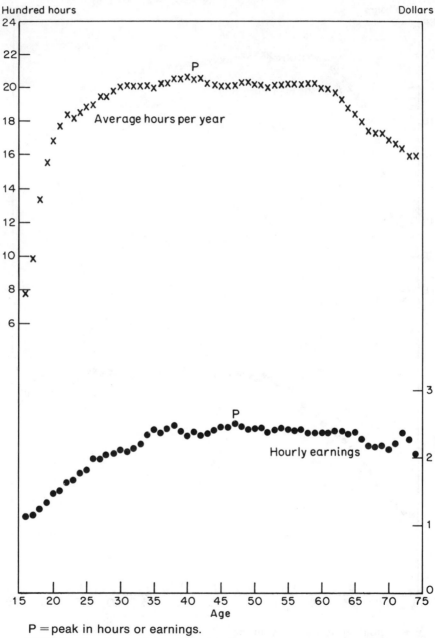

P = peak in hours or earnings.
SOURCE: See Appendix to this chapter.

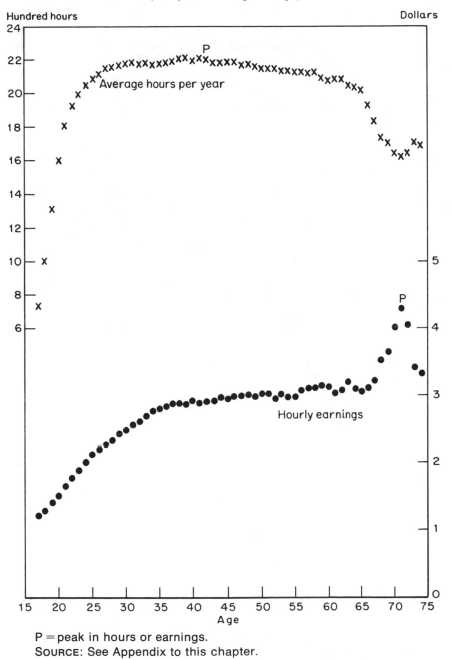

FIGURE 3.3
HOURLY EARNINGS AND AVERAGE HOURS PER YEAR, TOTAL UNITED STATES,
ALL EMPLOYED WHITE MEN, HIGH SCHOOL LEVEL
(five-year moving average)

P = peak in hours or earnings.
SOURCE: See Appendix to this chapter.

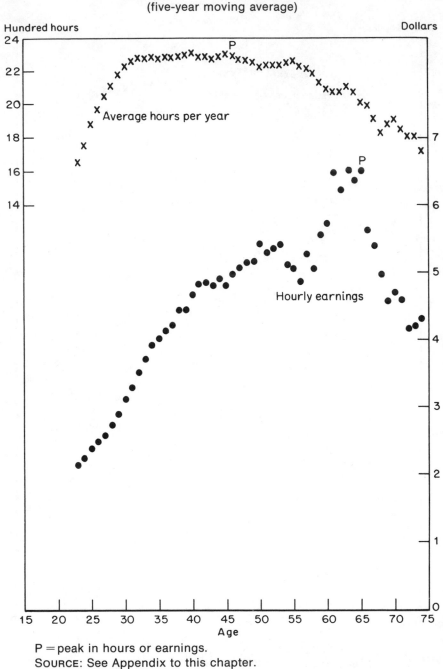

FIGURE 3.4
HOURLY EARNINGS AND AVERAGE HOURS PER YEAR, TOTAL UNITED STATES,
ALL EMPLOYED WHITE MEN, COLLEGE LEVEL
(five-year moving average)

P = peak in hours or earnings.
SOURCE: See Appendix to this chapter.

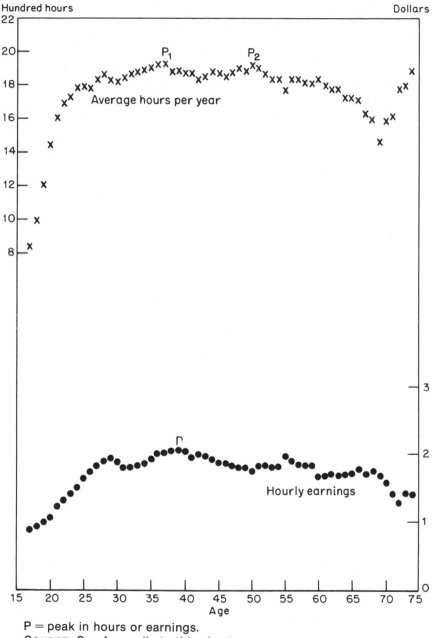

FIGURE 3.5
HOURLY EARNINGS AND AVERAGE HOURS PER YEAR, TOTAL UNITED STATES,
ALL EMPLOYED NONWHITE MEN, ALL EDUCATION LEVELS COMBINED
(five-year moving average)

P = peak in hours or earnings.
SOURCE: See Appendix to this chapter.

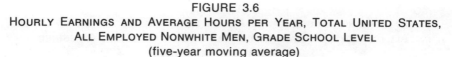

FIGURE 3.6
HOURLY EARNINGS AND AVERAGE HOURS PER YEAR, TOTAL UNITED STATES,
ALL EMPLOYED NONWHITE MEN, GRADE SCHOOL LEVEL
(five-year moving average)

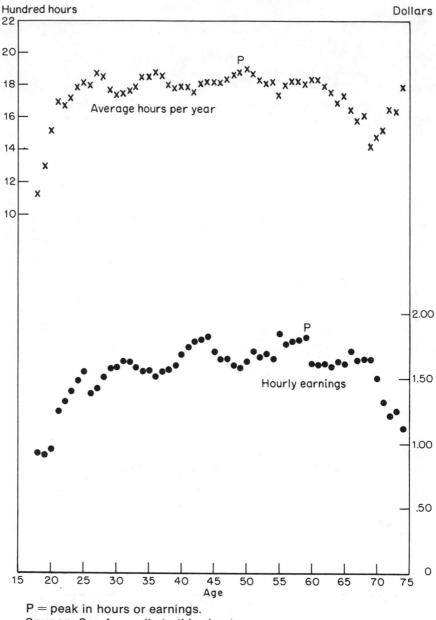

P = peak in hours or earnings.
SOURCE: See Appendix to this chapter.

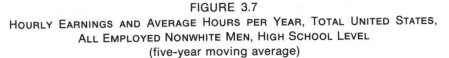

FIGURE 3.7

HOURLY EARNINGS AND AVERAGE HOURS PER YEAR, TOTAL UNITED STATES,
ALL EMPLOYED NONWHITE MEN, HIGH SCHOOL LEVEL
(five-year moving average)

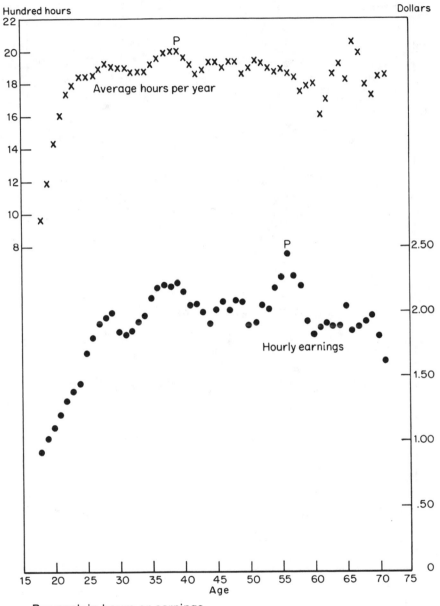

P = peak in hours or earnings.
SOURCE: See Appendix to this chapter.

FIGURE 3.8
Hourly Earnings and Average Hours per Year, Total United States, All Employed Nonwhite Men, College Level
(five-year moving average)

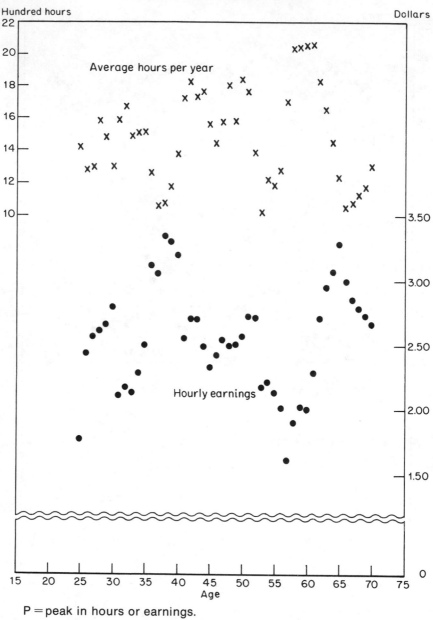

P = peak in hours or earnings.
Source: See Appendix to this chapter.

The theory developed in Chapter 1 predicts a relation between the allocation of time, wage rates, and other variables at different ages that can be tested with the data in the 1/1,000 sample. The prediction is that:

$$\log L_{tt'} = a_0 + a_1 \log w_{tt'} + a_2 \log w_{tt'}^0 + a_3 \log Z_{tt'} + a_4 t + a_5 \log v_{tt'},$$

$$(3.1)$$

where

$L_{tt'}$ = average number of hours allocated to consumption activities at time t' by the male cohort aged t;

$w_{tt'}$ = average wage rate at time t' of the male cohort aged t;

$w_{tt'}^0$ = average wage rate at time t' of other family members of the male cohort aged t;

$Z_{tt'}$ = average family size at time t' of the male cohort aged t;

$v_{tt'}$ = average income other than earnings at time t' of the male cohort aged t.

I have already indicated how the average wage rate, income other than earnings, and family size can be measured for men of different ages from the 1/1,000 sample. Since the information available for men does not give the average hours worked of other family members, I did not measure their wage rates, but instead used the difference between the average family income and own income of men as a measure of the total earnings of other family members.

The dependent variable in equation (3.1), hours spent at consumption, is very difficult to measure accurately. One simple approach follows the theory developed in the first part of Chapter 1 in assuming that time can be allocated only to work or consumption. Then the hours spent at consumption during any year would equal the difference between the total hours in a year and the hours spent at work: [3]

$$L_{tt'} = (52 \times 7 \times 24) - N_{tt'} = 8{,}736 - N_{tt'}. \qquad (3.2)$$

Although used in many of the following regressions, this measure has several obvious shortcomings. Some time, especially for younger persons, is generally spent neither producing nor consuming but investing in human capital (see the discussion in section 1.5, above).

---

3. Although there are 8,760 hours in a typical year, the figure 8,736 (= 52 × 168) is more consistent with the way hours worked are estimated.

The information available for each person in the 1/1,000 sample gives his years of schooling completed and whether he was enrolled in school (as of April 1960), but not how many hours he spent in school, in on-the-job training, or investing in other kinds of human capital. The errors in the estimates of consumption hours from the neglect of time spent in school can be reduced only if persons in each schooling class who are at least several years older than those typically completing that class are included: they must be at least age 18 if they have eight years or fewer of schooling, at least age 22 if they have nine to twelve years, and at least 26 if they have more than twelve.

In several studies it has been shown that a significant amount of time is usually spent in formal or informal on-the-job training, especially during the first ten years of labor force participation after completion of schooling.[4] Since the time spent in such training is generally reported to the Census as work, the estimates of hours worked are biased upward, especially at young ages. If, however, all training time were reported as work, the estimates of consumption hours spent derived from equation (3.2) would not be biased; if only some training time were not reported as work, estimated consumption hours would be biased upward, presumably especially at young ages. Since wage rates are estimated by dividing earnings by reported hours of work, they are biased downward, again especially at young ages.

A further problem is time lost due to ill health: this time and the time spent investing in health both tend to rise with age.[5] Hence, the estimates of consumption time derived from equation (3.2) would be biased upward, especially at older ages since, as Grossman shows, at least some of the time spent on health should be included along with time spent investing in human capital. The increase in the bias with age is usually small, however, below age 60.[6]

Time spent sleeping and in other "personal care" probably should be distinguished from other consumption time because

---

4. See especially Jacob Mincer, *Schooling, Experience, and Earnings* (New York: NBER, 1974).

5. See Michael Grossman, *The Demand for Health: A Theoretical and Empirical Investigation,* NBER Occasional Paper 119 (New York: NBER, 1972), Chap. 5.

6. An average of about 4.8 working days a year are spent in ill health between ages 17 and 24, 4.9 days between ages 25 and 44, and 6.3 days between ages 45 and 64 (U.S. Public Health Service, *Time Lost from Work Among the Currently Employed Population,* Series 10, no. 71, April 1972).

presumably goods cannot easily be substituted for time in the production of personal care, nor can other commodities easily be substituted for personal care itself. One piece of evidence supporting these presumptions is that sleeping time, a major part of personal care time, averages a little over 7½ hours per day in very different countries.[7] Another piece of evidence is that time spent on personal care by women working in the market sector is only slightly less than the approximately 75 hours a week spent by women not working there at all.[8]

A somewhat extreme assumption of no substitution possibilities in the production and consumption of personal care implies that the time spent producing personal care would be fixed, say at 70 hours per week or approximately 3,640 hours per year. The time spent producing other household commodities could be estimated from the equation,

$$L'_{tt'} = 8,736 - 3,640 - N_{tt'} = 5,096 - N_{tt'}; \tag{3.3}$$

and this estimate can be used in equation (3.1).

The theory developed in Chapter 1 predicts that if equation (3.1) is estimated from cross-sectional data of the kind found in the 1/1,000 sample, the parameter values would be, aside from sampling errors and measurement biases,

$$a_1 = -[(1 - s_1)\sigma_f + s_1\sigma_c] < 0;$$

$$a_2 = s_2(\sigma_f - \sigma_c) \gtreqless 0;$$

$$a_4 = r'\upsilon_c - [s_3 + (1 - s_3)\sigma_c]g_w; \tag{3.4}$$

where

σ_c = elasticity of substitution in consumption between commodities in different time periods;

σ_f = elasticity of substitution in production between any two inputs at a particular time;

r' = difference between current rate of interest and time preference;

7. See A. Szalar, "The Multinational Comparative Time Budget Research Project," *American Behavioral Scientist* (December 1966); Table 6 contains data for eleven countries, including the United States, the U.S.S.R., Bulgaria, France, Yugoslavia, and Germany.

8. See, for examples, ibid., Table 9.

s_1 = share of husband's time in cost of producing commodities;

s_2 = share of wife's time in cost of producing commodities;

s_3 = share of goods in cost of producing commodities: $s_3 = 1 - s_1 - s_2$;

g_w = rate of growth over time in real wage rate at given age.

Tables 3.1 and 3.2 give the results of running a wide variety of regressions with the 1/1,000 sample. Three-year moving averages of all the variables are used to reduce the effects of the large measurement errors in the original data. For purposes of comparison, however, some results using original data are also included in each table. Moving averages can be expected to introduce positive serial correlation into the residuals, and they clearly do here: the Durbin-Watson statistics are generally much lower for the regressions with moving averages than for those with original data. Moving averages can also result in spuriously high t statistics, and for this reason levels of significance are not given for the regression coefficients.

3.1   WHITES

Table 3.1 contains the results for all white males, and separately for those with eight years or less of schooling, nine–twelve years, and more than twelve years, when consumption time is estimated by equations (3.2) and (3.3). Almost all the regression coefficients for the own hourly wage rate are negative. The three positive coefficients, for college graduates, have low t values, whereas all the negative coefficients in the moving average regressions have very high t values. As would be expected since the coefficients are elasticities, the magnitudes estimated from consumption time net of the time spent on personal care are about two to three times larger than those estimated from all consumption time. Also, the coefficients estimated from moving averages are several times larger, in absolute value, than those estimated from original data.

Family size always has a negative coefficient for the three separate education classes, and these have t values exceeding 2.5 in more than half the cases. For all classes combined, two coefficients are positive but have very low t values; one is negative with a t value close to 2. The preponderance of negative coefficients suggests that an increase in family size results in an increase in time spent working by men.

In all cases but two, other family income, which is used as a measure of wage rates of other family members, have positive coefficients. The t values are negligible for the two negative coefficients and high for most of the positive ones. The preponderance of positive coefficients suggests that an increase in the wage rates of other family members reduces the time spent working by men.

The coefficients for age are positive for the three education classes when only age and the man's wage rate are included, and negative when all the variables are included. The coefficients are positive for all classes combined when moving averages are used. Most of the negative coefficients have low t values, whereas most of the positive ones have sizable t values. Over-all, there is no clear indication of the nature of the effect of age on the allocation of time.

Income other than earnings always has a positive coefficient. However, most of the t values are small, and more importantly, practically all the coefficients are themselves small: five are 0.01 or less, and only one is above 0.025. In contrast, five coefficients for the male wage rate are above 0.20.

The negative coefficient for the own (i.e., male) wage rate is predicted by the theory developed in Chapter 1. An increase in own wage at any age reduces own time allocated to consumption at that age because of substitutions toward goods and other person's time in the production of commodities and substitution toward commodities at other ages. The elasticity of response of own time—i.e., the regression coefficient for own wage—is predicted to be a weighted average of the elasticities of substitution in production and consumption, the weights being the shares of own time and other inputs in production costs [see equation (3.4)].

The coefficient for own wage rate is about −0.12 in the regression combining all education classes when total consumption time is included, and it more than doubles (to about −0.27) when estimated time spent on personal care is excluded. Although the sizable difference between these coefficients is arithmetically necessary, I believe it also reflects the much smaller elasticity of substitution in production and consumption for personal care than for other commodities. The estimate of 0.27 suggests that the average of the elasticities of substitution in production and consumption is significantly greater than zero and smaller than 1.

The true average of these elasticities may be even larger than

TABLE 3.1
REGRESSIONS FOR CONSUMPTION TIME OF WHITE MEN: LEVEL EQUATIONS

Form of Dependent Variable [a] (in logs)	Intercept	Age	Log Hourly Earnings	Log Other Income	Log Other Family Income	Log Family Size	Mult. Corr. Coeff.	Adj. R^2	Durbin-Watson
All Education Levels; Ages 22–65; Three-year Moving Average									
5,096 − HW/YR	8.176 (643.0)	0.002 (11.27)	−0.260 (15.81)				.92	.85	0.45
5,096 − HW/YR	7.881 (79.95)	0.002 (2.03)	−0.275 (4.09)	0.017 (1.26)	0.024 (2.27)	0.038 (0.81)	.94	.87	0.49
8,736 − HW/YR	8.978 (1520.)	0.001 (11.10)	−0.118 (15.66)				.93	.85	0.45
8,736 − HW/YR	8.743 (192.9)	0.001 (0.13)	−0.128 (0.14)	0.007 (1.20)	0.011 (2.24)	0.020 (0.91)	.94	.87	0.49
All Education Levels; Ages 22–65; Original Data									
5,096 − HW/YR	7.925 (65.79)	−0.001 (0.52)	−0.083 (1.31)	0.007 (0.67)	0.035 (2.79)	−0.089 (1.91)	.89	.77	1.20
Grade School; Ages 18–65; Three-year Moving Average									
5,096 − HW/YR	8.216 (469.4)	0.001 (3.60)	−0.266 (9.45)				.83	.68	0.79
5,096 − HW/YR	7.828 (36.76)	−0.001 (0.76)	−0.167 (3.01)	0.016 (1.05)	0.045 (2.25)	−0.021 (0.56)	.86	.70	0.68
8,736 − HW/YR	8.900 (1075.)	0.0004 (3.58)	−0.126 (9.48)				.83	.69	0.78
8,736 − HW/YR	8.709 (86.64)	−0.0003 (0.081)	−0.081 (3.09)	0.008 (1.06)	0.022 (2.29)	−0.007 (0.42)	.86	.70	0.68

Independent Variables (t values in parentheses)

Grade School; Ages 18–65; Original Data

5,096 − HW/YR	7.937 (46.42)	−0.003 (3.21)	−0.001 (0.01)	0.0002 (0.02)	0.053 (3.10)	−0.123 (2.97)	.74	.49	1.40

High School; Ages 22–65; Three-year Moving Average

5,096 − HW/YR	8.139 (785.5)	0.003 (11.7)	−0.253 (15.21)				.92	.85	0.55
5,096 − HW/YR	7.995 (104.3)	−0.001 (0.84)	−0.167 (3.19)	0.040 (4.26)	0.006 (0.69)	−0.042 (1.77)	.95	.89	0.68
8,736 − HW/YR	8.861 (1890.)	0.001 (11.6)	−0.114 (15.16)				.92	.84	0.54
8,736 − HW/YR	8.796 (252.2)	−0.0004 (0.76)	−0.077 (3.24)	0.018 (4.21)	0.003 (0.67)	−0.018 (1.66)	.95	.89	0.67

High School; Ages 22–65; Original Data

5,096 − HW/YR	7.889 (83.83)	−0.002 (1.72)	−0.046 (0.87)	0.022 (2.61)	0.027 (2.67)	−0.079 (2.87)	.85	.69	1.66

College; Ages 26–65; Three-year Moving Average

5,096 − HW/YR	8.106 (374.6)	0.004 (6.71)	−0.225 (7.94)				.79	.61	0.60
5,096 − HW/YR	8.265 (85.50)	−0.004 (2.68)	0.050 (0.73)	0.022 (2.10)	−0.006 (0.55)	−0.224 (4.59)	.91	.80	0.64
8,736 − HW/YR	8.845 (913.4)	0.002 (6.66)	−0.100 (7.89)				.79	.61	0.60
8,736 − HW/YR	8.916 (205.2)	−0.002 (2.67)	0.022 (0.72)	0.010 (2.10)	−0.003 (0.55)	−0.100 (4.54)	.90	.79	0.64

College; Ages 26–65; Original Data

5,096 − HW/YR	8.205 (71.25)	−0.004 (2.90)	0.063 (1.16)	0.013 (1.37)	0.004 (0.29)	−0.214 (4.89)	.81	.60	1.39

Source: 1/1,000 sample of U.S. Census, 1960.

a. Total hours in a year = 8,736 (= 52 × 168); total hours net of time spent in personal care = 5,096 (= 52 × 70); HW/YR = hours of work per year. For further clarification, see equations (3.2) and (3.3).

0.27 because random errors of measurement in the own wage rate bias its regression coefficient toward zero and even toward positive values. Measurement errors in total earnings bias the wage rate estimates but presumably not hours. The consequence is that the regression coefficient is biased toward zero. Random errors of measurement in hours worked bias the estimates of wage rates and consumption hours in the same direction; hence, the regression coefficient is biased toward a positive value. The importance of measurement error can be seen by comparing the results using moving averages with those using the original data. Presumably a moving average reduces the importance of measurement error because positive and negative errors are averaged together. The own wage coefficient is much higher in all the regressions using moving averages than in those using the original data (except for the college-educated group, where they are about equal).[9] Some independent evidence that errors of measurement reduce (in absolute value) the own wage coefficient is found in the regressions using hours of work as the dependent variable (see the discussion of Tables 3.5, 3.6, and 3.7).

Systematic errors in the own wage rate bias its regression coefficient, with the major bias probably due to the inclusion in measured working hours of time spent in on-the-job training. Since more time is spent in such training at younger ages (relative to working time), the rate of increase in the measured wage rate exceeds that in the true wage rate;[10] therefore, its coefficient would be biased toward zero. Moreover, if actual working time enters into the production of human capital,[11] the true wage rate would understate the shadow price of time, again especially at younger ages. Hence, even the regression coefficient for the true wage rate would be biased toward zero relative to the coefficient for the shadow price of time.[12]

---

9. Of course, the bias in the own-wage coefficient depends not only on its measurement error, but also on those in other independent variables, on the partial correlation between these variables and the own wage, and on the true values of the other regression coefficients—see E. Malinvaud, *Statistical Methods of Econometrics* (Chicago: Rand McNally, 1966), Chap. 10. The difference between values of the coefficients based on moving averages and those based on original data suggests that the net effect of *all* the errors is to bias the coefficient for own wage toward zero.

10. In other language, the increase in the "net" wage rate exceeds the increase in wage rate "capacity."

11. See the formulation in section 1.5, above.

12. Other biases result from the inclusion in consumption time of some time spent in school, job search, portfolio management, and investment in health. Their net effect is probably to bias the own wage coefficient away from zero.

The own wage coefficient is very similar in all the regressions in Table 3.1 when age and own wage are the only independent variables; there is a slight tendency for it to decline with increases in education. When the other independent variables are entered, the own wage coefficient for each of the separate education classes is reduced substantially (but not the one combining all classes). It remains about the same for persons with elementary and high school education, and becomes positive and with a very low t value for persons with a college education.

The positive coefficient for my measure of the wage rates of other family members implies according to the theory [see equation (3.4)] that the elasticity of substitution in production exceeds the elasticity of substitution in consumption, which is consistent with the evidence on consumption analyzed by Ghez in Chapter 2. The coefficients are always rather small, never above $+0.06$, but their size cannot be taken seriously since this measure of other wage rates has large random and even systematic errors.[13]

An increase in family size apparently reduces the consumption time of men (increases their working time); the elasticity of response, although generally small, is positively related to education. Ghez finds that the consumption of goods is strongly and positively related to family size (section 2.5, above); moreover, a finding of many studies is that the labor force participation of married women, perhaps especially college-educated women, is significantly reduced if the household includes young children.[14] One plausible interpretation of these results (see section 1.7) is that child care uses a woman's time much more intensively than a man's, perhaps especially among the college educated.[15]

All the age coefficients are positive when only age and the own wage rate are entered in the regressions; this is also shown graphically in Figures 3.1–3.8, where hours worked peak at an earlier age

---

13. Note, however, that James Smith, using other data and a much better measure of the wage rate of wives, also finds small positive coefficients; see his, "The Life Cycle Allocation of Time in a Family Context" (Ph.D. diss., University of Chicago, 1972).

14. See, for example, Smith, ibid., and Arleen Leibowitz, "Women's Allocation of Time to Market and Non-Market Activities" (Ph.D. diss., Columbia University, 1972). Ghez finds only a weak relation between education and the elasticity of response of the consumption of goods to a change in family size.

15. This interpretation is elaborated in Smith, "Life Cycle Allocation," Chap. IV, to explain why the working time of men actually increases as family size increases.

than own wage rate. When the other independent variables are entered, however, the age coefficients become negative (but with low *t* values) in the regressions for the separate education classes, but not for all classes combined. According to the theory developed in Chapter 1, the age coefficient in a regression using observations of a given cohort over its life cycle would equal the product of the elasticity of substitution in consumption and the difference between the rate of interest and the time preference for the present. The coefficient in a regression using observations across successive cohorts, such as those found in the Census, would be "biased" downward by a growth in real wage rates between cohorts (see the discussion by Ghez in section 2.3); the bias would be sizable if the growth in wage rates and the share of goods in commodity production costs were sizable [see equation (3.4)]. Therefore, the mixture of positive and negative signs for the age coefficient does not necessarily imply that age has little systematic effect on the allocation of time. Indeed, the analysis in Chapter 4 suggests that the consumption of both time and goods rises significantly with age.

An increase in income other than earnings appears to increase consumption time, although the elasticity of response is small. For all schooling levels combined and for grade school men, it is only one-tenth of the elasticity of response of consumption time to an increase in the own wage rate; for high school men, it is about one-fourth. These results are generally consistent, therefore, with the implication of our theory that life cycle variations in wage rates have a more important effect than life cycle variations in other income. Indeed, the theory implies that if each cohort accurately foresees the future, life cycle variations in other income have *no* effect on the allocation of time. Since the regression coefficients for other income are small and generally have low *t* values, these results are not grossly inconsistent with accurate *cohort* forecasts of other income. On the other hand, since the coefficients are always positive even though the large errors of measurement in other income presumably bias them toward zero, and since Ghez finds sizable coefficients for other income in his regression for goods (see Chapter 2), cohorts may be systematically adapting their forecasts of income to unexpected changes in observed values.[16]

---

16. If the wealth elasticity of consumption time equals 1, and if nonhuman wealth is about one-quarter of all wealth, the true value of the regression coefficient of other income would equal $+(\frac{1}{4})a$, where *a* is the percentage increase in expected nonhuman

3.2 NONWHITES

Corresponding regression results for all male nonwhites and for those with an elementary school, high school, and college education are presented in Table 3.2. Since the number of nonwhites in the 1/1,000 sample is only about one-tenth the number of whites, some nonwhite cell sizes are quite small. For example, an average of only 7 observations of nonwhites with a college education and 25 observations of nonwhites with a high school education are found at each age (see Table 3A.1, below). One would expect, therefore, random errors of measurement and other "noise" to have an even greater effect on the results for nonwhites than they do for whites, which is apparently true. For example, all the correlation coefficients are considerably smaller for nonwhites than for whites. In the original data, where noise is more important, the coefficient of determination for all nonwhite men is only about one-fifth, whereas for all whites it is almost four-fifths.[17]

In spite of the importance of measurement error and other noise, the results for nonwhites are qualitatively very close to those for whites and to the predictions of the theory. In Table 3.3, to facilitate comparison I show each coefficient for nonwhites alongside the corresponding coefficient for whites. The own-wage-rate coefficients for both nonwhites and whites are negative (except for college persons), have reasonably high *t* values, and are about the same for all elementary and high school men for both whites and nonwhites. The nonwhite coefficients are considerably smaller than the white ones, possibly because of the greater measurement error in the nonwhite data.[18]

---

wealth adapted from an observed 1 per cent increase in other income. If the values generally observed for this coefficient (less than $+0.02$) were close to the true values, *a* would be less than 0.08, a very small adaptation coefficient.

Moreover, note that other income is not exogenous: its lifetime pattern is partly a consequence of the optimal lifetime patterns for goods and time operating through the effect of the latter two on savings and the accumulation of nonhuman capital. In these regressions, therefore, other income may pick up the effect of omitted determinants of the lifetime allocation of time. Even the direction of the resulting bias in the coefficient of other income is not obvious, however, partly because there is usually not even a monotonic relation between the optimal path of consumption time and that of nonhuman capital.

17. I cannot explain why the serial correlation for the residuals in the regressions for nonwhites is much less than for the residuals for whites.

18. The importance of measurement error is further emphasized by the regressions for nonwhites using the original data. Although these own-wage coefficients are also negative, they are negligible and have negligible *t* values.

TABLE 3.2
REGRESSIONS FOR CONSUMPTION TIME OF NONWHITE MEN: LEVEL EQUATIONS

Form of Dependent Variable[a] (in logs)	Inter-cept	Age	Log Hourly Earnings	Log Other Income	Log Other Family Income	Log Family Size	Mult. Corr. Coeff.	Adj. R^2	Durbin-Watson
All Education Levels; Ages 22–65; Three-year Moving Average									
5,096 — HW/YR	8.144 (612.9)	0.0002 (0.76)	-0.106 (4.88)				.61	.34	0.94
5,096 — HW/YR	8.008 (64.11)	-0.001 (1.98)	-0.051 (2.25)	0.003 (0.89)	0.033 (2.42)	-0.087 (3.42)	.78	.55	1.24
8,736 — HW/YR	8.865 (1412.)	0.0001 (0.77)	-0.050 (4.90)				.61	.34	0.94
8,736 — HW/YR	8.802 (149.2)	-0.003 (1.97)	-0.025 (2.28)	0.002 (0.88)	0.015 (2.40)	-0.041 (3.42)	.78	.55	1.23
All Education Levels; Ages 22–65; Original Data									
5,096 — HW/YR	8.104 (41.01)	-0.001 (2.00)	-0.008 (0.21)	0.010 (1.97)	0.018 (0.85)	-0.107 (2.46)	.53	.19	2.17
Grade School; Ages 18–65; Three-year Moving Average									
5,096 — HW/YR	8.150 (553.5)	0.0000 (0.12)	-0.110 (3.23)				.52	.24	0.83
5,096 — HW/YR	7.791 (51.87)	-0.0004 (0.40)	-0.048 (1.35)	-0.005 (0.74)	0.054 (3.65)	-0.016 (0.26)	.68	.39	0.99
8,736 — HW/YR	8.869 (1242.)	0.0000 (0.14)	-0.054 (3.29)				.53	.24	0.83
8,736 — HW/YR	8.695 (119.1)	-0.0002 (0.36)	-0.024 (1.41)	-0.002 (0.75)	0.026 (3.61)	-0.007 (0.23)	.68	.39	0.99

Independent Variables (t values in parentheses)

Grade School; Ages 18–65; Original Data

	Constant								
5,096 — HW/YR	7.706 (46.32)	−0.001 (1.38)	−0.012 (0.26)	0.001 (0.19)	0.048 (2.68)	−0.063 (0.99)	.43	.09	2.14

High School; Ages 22–65; Three-year Moving Average

	Constant								
5,096 — HW/YR	8.117 (528.9)	0.0002 (0.40)	−0.079 (3.20)				.48	.20	1.04
5,096 — HW/YR	7.923 (66.03)	−0.001 (1.18)	−0.042 (1.55)	0.011 (2.17)	0.027 (1.96)	−0.040 (1.22)	.60	.28	1.22
8,736 — HW/YR	8.852 (1244.)	0.0001 (0.44)	−0.038 (3.26)				.49	.20	1.05
8,736 — HW/YR	8.764 (157.4)	−0.0003 (1.16)	−0.020 (1.61)	0.005 (2.17)	0.013 (1.93)	−0.019 (1.23)	.61	.28	1.23

High School; Ages 22–65; Original Data

	Constant								
5,096 — HW/YR	8.137 (76.67)	−0.001 (0.73)	−0.003 (0.06)	0.001 (0.14)	−0.005 (0.54)	−0.008 (0.17)	.16	−.11	1.82

College; Ages 26–65; Three-year Moving Average

	Constant								
5,096 — HW/YR	8.140 (122.7)	−0.004 (2.63)	0.046 (0.67)				.45	.14	0.69
5,096 — HW/YR	7.705 (41.12)	−0.004 (4.33)	0.105 (2.00)	0.006 (0.63)	0.078 (3.39)	−0.148 (3.05)	.80	.57	1.22
8,736 — HW/YR	8.868 (284.9)	−0.002 (2.63)	0.021 (0.66)				.45	.15	0.68
8,736 — HW/YR	8.660 (98.92)	−0.002 (4.36)	0.049 (2.00)	0.003 (0.63)	0.037 (3.40)	−0.070 (3.08)	.80	.57	0.22

College; Ages 26–65; Original Data

	Constant								
5,096 — HW/YR	7.830 (26.93)	−0.003 (1.37)	0.265 (3.78)	0.001 (0.10)	0.047 (1.54)	−0.187 (1.93)	.70	.35	2.15

SOURCE: Same as Table 3.1. See also section 2 of the appendix to this chapter.
a. See Table 3.1, note a.

TABLE 3.3
COMPARISON OF REGRESSION COEFFICIENTS
FOR WHITES AND NONWHITES[a]

Dependent Variable [b] (in logs)	Age	Log Hourly Earnings	Log Other Income	Log Other Family Income	Log Family Size
All Education Levels; Ages 22–65; Three-year Moving Average					
5,096 − HW/YR	.002	−.260			
	.0002	−.106			
5,096 − HW/YR	.002	−.275	.017	.024	.038
	−.001	−.051	.003	.033	−.087
8,736 − HW/YR	.001	−.118			
	.0001	−.050			
8,736 − HW/YR	.001	−.128	.007	.011	.020
	−.003	−.025	.002	.015	−.041
All Education Levels; Ages 22–65; Original Data					
5,096 − HW/YR	−.001	−.083	.007	.035	−.089
	−.001	−.008	.010	.018	−.107
Grade School; Ages 18–65; Three-year Moving Average					
5,096 − HW/YR	.001	−.266			
	.0000	−.110			
5,096 − HW/YR	−.001	−.167	.016	.045	−.021
	−.0004	−.048	−.005	.054	−.016
8,736 − HW/YR	.0004	−.126			
	.0000	−.054			
8,736 − HW/YR	−.0003	−.081	.008	.022	−.007
	−.0002	−.024	−.002	.026	−.007
Grade School; Ages 18–65; Original Data					
5,096 − HW/YR	−.003	−.001	.0002	.053	−.123
	−.001	−.021	.001	.048	−.063
High School; Ages 22–65; Three-year Moving Average					
5,096 − HW/YR	.003	−.253			
	.0002	−.079			
5,096 − HW/YR	−.001	−.167	.040	.006	−.042
	−.001	−.042	.011	.027	−.040
8,736 − HW/YR	.001	−.114			
	.0001	−.038			
8,736 − HW/YR	−.0004	−.077	.018	.003	−.018
	−.0003	−.020	.005	.013	−.019

TABLE 3.3 (continued)

Dependent Variable [b] (in logs)	Age	Log Hourly Earnings	Log Other Income	Log Other Family Income	Log Family Size
High School; Ages 22–65; Original Data					
5,096 − HW/YR	−.002	−.046	.022	.027	−.079
	−.001	−.003	.001	−.005	−.008
College; Ages 26–65; Three-year Moving Average					
5,096 − HW/YR	.004	−.225			
	−.004	.046			
5,096 − HW/YR	−.004	.050	.022	−.006	−.224
	−.004	.105	.006	.078	−.148
8,736 − HW/YR	.002	−.100			
	−.002	.021			
8,736 − HW/YR	−.002	.022	.010	−.003	−.100
	−.002	.049	.003	.037	−.070
College; Ages 26–65; Original Data					
5,096 − HW/YR	−.004	.063	.013	.004	−.214
	−.003	.265	.001	.047	−.187

SOURCE: Same as Table 3.1.
a. Upper coefficient in each cell is for whites; lower one is for nonwhites.
b. See Table 3.1, note a.

My measure of the wage rates of other family members always has a positive coefficient that is typically almost as large (in absolute value) for nonwhites as the own wage coefficient. Therefore, nonwhite men also work less in the market sector when their wives' wage rate increases. Perhaps nonwhite men allocate less of their time and nonwhite women more of their time to the market sector than do white men and women,[19] because the difference in wage rates between men and women is smaller in nonwhite than in white families.[20]

19. Nonwhite men averaged 1,900 hours of work in 1959, whereas white men averaged 2,147 hours; similarly, nonwhite women averaged 1,385 and white women averaged 1,486 (Smith, "Life Cycle Allocation," Table 4, p. 33).

20. Similarly, married men allocate more time and married women less time to the market sector than do unmarried men and women. See U.S. Census of Population, 1960: vol. 2, Subject Reports, Part 6A, Employment Status and Work Experience (1963), Tables 4 and 12.

Family size consistently has a negative coefficient, with a high *t* value for all schooling levels combined and for college-educated nonwhite men. The coefficients for whites and nonwhites are about equal in the three separate education classes. Apparently, an increase in family size also induces nonwhite men to spend more time and nonwhite women less time at work.[21]

The age coefficients for nonwhites, like those for whites, are small, not consistently positive or negative, and have small *t* values. Perhaps negative values are more frequent for nonwhites, but the difference is of little significance. As mentioned earlier, the age coefficient is biased downward; therefore, a small age coefficient is not evidence that age has little effect on the allocation of time.

The coefficient for other income of nonwhites is generally positive and has a low *t* value. Its size relative to the own wage coefficient is about the same for all whites and nonwhites, and for whites and nonwhites with an elementary school education. Hence, there is a suggestion that both nonwhites and whites moderately adapt their expectations of other income to unexpected changes in observed values.

James Smith ran regressions similar to those in Tables 3.1 and 3.2 on a completely independent body of data for a different year; namely, the 1967 Survey of Economic Opportunity. A comparison of his results with mine, reported in Table 3.4, offers an important opportunity to check the validity of my findings. The coefficient of the male wage rate is always negative in his regressions; it is very similar to mine for all whites and for those with a high school education; it is (absolutely) larger than mine for all blacks[22] and for whites with a college education, and smaller than mine for whites with an elementary school education. His measure of the wage rate of wives is much better than mine, and it is reassuring to my emphasis on measurement error to note that his coefficient is also larger (except for whites with an elementary school education) than mine. The coefficient of his family size variable is more consistently negative, probably because he uses the number of children under age seven

---

21. Note, however, that the effect of family size on the working time of nonwhite women is considerably less than that for white women (see Smith, "Life Cycle Allocation," Chap. IV).

22. His data refer only to blacks, mine to all nonwhites; the differences between these groups are not large.

TABLE 3.4
COMPARISON OF REGRESSIONS BY SMITH AND BECKER [a]
FOR HOURLY WAGE RATES OF MEN
(*t* values are in parentheses)

	Hourly Wage of Men	Wages of Wife [b]	Age	Family Size [c]
All whites				
Becker	−0.128	0.011	0.001	0.020
	(4.14)	(2.24)	(2.13)	(0.91)
Smith	−0.1040	0.0202	0.00014	−0.0178
	(6.88)	(0.82)	(0.67)	(4.60)
Whites; college				
Becker	0.022	−0.003	−0.002	−0.100
	(0.72)	(0.55)	(2.67)	(4.54)
Smith	−0.0405	0.0195	−0.00002	−0.0092
	(2.24)	(1.17)	(0.041)	(1.13)
Whites; high school				
Becker	−0.077	0.003	−0.00004	−0.018
	(3.24)	(0.67)	(0.76)	(1.66)
Smith	−0.0852	0.0510	−0.00003	−0.0198
	(4.16)	(2.10)	(0.097)	(4.02)
Whites; elementary school				
Becker	−0.081	0.022	−0.0003	−0.0007
	(0.09)	(2.29)	(0.68)	(0.42)
Smith	−0.0029	−0.0415	0.009	0.0072
	(0.084)	(1.92)	(2.08)	(0.92)
All blacks				
Becker	−0.025	0.015	−0.041	−0.003
	(2.28)	(2.40)	(3.42)	(1.97)
Smith	−0.0643	0.0455	0.00001	−0.0107
	(2.16)	(1.71)	(0.031)	(1.35)

SOURCE: See accompanying text.

a. Becker's regressions include one additional variable — other nonlabor income.

b. Becker's variable is other family income.

c. Becker's variable is family size, while Smith's is number of children younger than age seven.

rather than total family size. The participation of married women in the labor force is also more sensitive to the number of children under age seven than to the total number of children.[23]

3.3   WORKING TIME

For comparability with studies that use working time rather than consumption time, I ran regressions like those in Tables 3.1 and 3.2 with working time as the dependent variable; the results are presented in Tables 3.5 and 3.6. Since the change in working time is, by definition, equal but opposite in sign to the change in consumption time, each coefficient in Tables 3.5 and 3.6 should be opposite in sign to the corresponding coefficient in Tables 3.1 and 3.3. Moreover, since average hours worked are about 30 per cent of all consumption hours and 70 per cent of consumption hours net of personal care,[24] the absolute value of a coefficient in Table 3.1 should be about three-tenths of the corresponding coefficient in Table 3.5[25] for all consumption time and seven-tenths for consumption time net of personal care.[26] The signs and magnitudes of the coefficients in Tables 3.5 and 3.6 generally do follow this pattern.

Since all the coefficients in Tables 3.1 and 3.2 were discussed earlier, I now consider only those for earnings in Tables 3.5 and 3.6. For whites, the coefficient of hourly earnings is positive and has a high t value except for college persons, for whom it is negative and has a low t value. Moreover, the coefficient declines as education increases. For nonwhites, the coefficient is also positive, again

---

23. See Smith, "Life Cycle Allocation," Chap. IV.

24. Since all white males worked about 2,100 hours in 1959 (see Table 3A.2), then $2,100/(8,736 - 2,100) = 0.32$, and $2,100/(5,096 - 2,100) = .70$.

25. Since the ratios for nonwhites are $1,833/(8,736 - 1,833) = 0.26$, and $1,833/(5,096 - 1,833) = 0.55$, coefficients in Table 3.2 should be about one-fourth and one-half of the corresponding coefficients in Table 3.6.

26. Since $dN = -dL$, where dL is the change in consumption time and dN is the change in working time,

$$\frac{dN}{N} = d \log N = \frac{-dL}{L} \frac{L}{N} = -d \log L \frac{L}{N}.$$

If $r = L/N$ is treated as a constant, by integration $\log N = -r \log L$. Therefore, if $\log L = \Sigma a_i \log X_i$, then by substitution, $\log N = \Sigma a_i' \log X_i$, where $a_i' = -ra_i$.

except for college persons; is much smaller than that for whites; and does not vary systematically with education.

In most studies, a negative rather than a positive relation has been found between hours worked and the own wage rate, and the negative relation has been interpreted as evidence that the income effect is more powerful than the substitution effect.[27] I obtain a positive relation partly because the income effect is reduced and perhaps largely eliminated by using life cycle observations, and partly because errors of measurement have been reduced. Wage rates usually are not directly observed but are constructed from presumably statistically independent observations on earnings and hours worked. As pointed out earlier, random errors of measurement in earnings bias the regression coefficient between hours worked and the constructed wage rate toward zero, whereas random errors in hours worked bias it toward -1. These biases would be especially large in small samples that are analyzed in disaggregated form.[28] Although the Census sample is large, it is obtained by inexperienced interviewers. Moreover, the sample is classified into more than 250 cells, and some have few observations: for example, nonwhite males with a college education average only seven observations at each age (and their wage rate has a negative coefficient [29]).

I tried to reduce the measurement error by using three-year moving averages of all the variables. The coefficient of hourly earnings is significantly larger algebraically, especially for whites, in these regressions than in those using the original data. The effect of measurement error can be reduced even further by using annual rather

---

27. See, for example, James A. Morgan et al., *Productive Americans* (Ann Arbor: University of Michigan Press, 1966).

28. For example, Morgan, *Productive Americans* (p. 21, n. 4), uses a sample of 2,214 men obtained by interviews and does not aggregate at all. However, he is aware of the biasing effect of measurement error in hours of work, but considers it not of dominant importance.

29. The wage rate coefficient is also negative for male whites with a college education, although they average 165 observations at each age (a smaller number of observations, however, than at the other two education classes). The coefficient is negative for both white and nonwhite college persons perhaps also because hours of work are less accurately measured for them. Men with less than a college education are usually paid on an hourly basis and a written record is kept of their hours, whereas college-educated men are usually salaried or self-employed and do not have their hours recorded so diligently.

TABLE 3.5
Regressions for Annual Hours Worked of White Men: Level Equations
(dependent variable = log annual hours worked = HW/YR)

		Independent Variables (t values in parentheses)					Mult. Corr. Coeff.	Adj. R^2	Durbin-Watson
Inter-cept	Age	Log Annual Earnings	Log Hourly Earnings	Log Other Income	Log Other Family Income	Log Family Size			
All Education Levels; Ages 22–65; Three-year Moving Average									
7.391 (373.4)	−0.003 (10.46)		0.386 (15.06)				.92	.84	0.43
7.843 (51.07)	−0.004 (2.45)		0.448 (4.28)	−0.020 (0.96)	−0.036 (2.17)	−0.091 (1.25)	.94	.86	0.50
5.251 (47.83)	−0.003 (12.57)	0.288 (21.91)					.96	.92	0.43
4.545 (13.69)	−0.004 (5.23)	0.424 (10.17)		−0.024 (1.87)	−0.008 (0.75)	−0.160 (4.12)	.98	.94	0.60
All Education Levels; Ages 22–65; Original Data									
5.342 (11.34)	−0.003 (2.46)	0.317 (5.39)		−0.013 (1.04)	−0.023 (1.45)	−0.067 (1.19)	.93	.85	1.68
Grade School; Ages 18–65; Three-year Moving Average									
7.268 (223.6)	−0.002 (3.46)		0.490 (9.39)				.83	.68	0.73
8.131 (20.83)	0.001 (0.31)		0.345 (3.38)	−0.033 (1.13)	−0.089 (2.45)	−0.018 (0.26)	.86	.71	0.68
4.593 (25.54)	−0.001 (4.83)	0.364 (16.34)					.93	.87	0.79
4.508 (8.44)	−0.003 (2.40)	0.401 (8.83)		0.001 (0.04)	−0.007 (0.26)	−0.085 (1.95)	.94	.87	0.92

Grade School; Ages 18–65; Original Data

5.708 (9.55)	0.0001 (0.05)	0.253 (4.03)	−0.0002 (0.01)	−0.037 (1.29)	0.024 (0.36)	.82	.63	2.09
High School; Ages 22–65; Three-year Moving Average								
7.457 (496.9)	−0.004 (11.40)		0.360 (14.97)			.92	.84	0.53
7.662 (67.58)	0.001 (0.52)	0.236 (3.40)	−0.055 (4.02)	−0.008 (0.59)	0.046 (1.30)	.95	.88	0.64
5.405 (51.15)	−0.003 (14.34)	0.274 (21.35)				.96	.92	0.53
5.189 (13.63)	−0.002 (1.49)	0.308 (7.24)	−0.032 (2.91)	0.010 (1.05)	−0.020 (0.74)	.97	.93	0.64
High School; Ages 22–65; Original Data								
6.072 (12.82)	−0.001 (0.63)	0.213 (3.88)	−0.020 (1.83)	−0.017 (1.31)	0.017 (0.47)	.89	.77	1.67
College; Ages 26–65; Three-year Moving Average								
7.512 (251.5)	−0.005 (6.49)		0.302 (7.73)			.79	.60	0.59
7.303 (53.71)	0.006 (2.62)	−0.068 (0.70)	−0.031 (2.08)	0.008 (0.51)	0.302 (4.39)	.90	.78	0.63
5.564 (29.86)	−0.004 (8.86)	0.257 (11.51)				.88	.77	0.63
5.770 (9.65)	−0.001 (0.53)	0.216 (2.64)	−0.038 (2.94)	0.025 (1.78)	0.058 (0.74)	.92	.82	0.76
College; Ages 26–65; Original Data								
6.560 (11.82)	0.001 (0.30)	0.109 (1.52)	−0.021 (1.73)	0.013 (0.78)	0.132 (1.82)	.81	.61	1.36

Source: See Table 3.1.

TABLE 3.6
REGRESSIONS FOR ANNUAL HOURS WORKED OF NONWHITE MEN: LEVEL EQUATIONS

Independent Variables (t values in parentheses)

Intercept	Age	Log Annual Earnings	Log Hourly Earnings	Log Other Income	Log Other Family Income	Log Family Size	Mult. Corr. Coeff.	Adj. R²	Durbin-Watson
All Education Levels; Ages 22–65; Three-year Moving Average									
7.417 (315.7)	−0.0003 (0.79)		0.193 (5.02)				.62	.35	0.95
7.640 (34.40)	0.001 (1.94)		0.098 (2.42)	−0.005 (0.83)	−0.056 (2.33)	0.153 (3.40)	.78	.55	1.23
5.946 (28.64)	−0.0003 (1.12)	0.196 (7.56)					.76	.56	0.99
6.480 (17.08)	0.001 (1.59)	0.135 (4.21)		−0.002 (0.41)	−0.034 (1.55)	0.126 (3.08)	.83	.65	1.24
All Education Levels; Ages 22–65; Original Data									
6.173 (10.63)	0.001 (1.48)	0.149 (2.74)		−0.017 (1.99)	−0.005 (0.14)	0.141 (1.95)	.63	.32	2.20
Grade School; Ages 18–65; Three-year Moving Average									
7.381 (233.5)	−0.0002 (0.24)		0.258 (3.52)				.55	.27	0.84
8.151 (24.81)	0.0001 (0.06)		0.131 (1.69)	0.010 (0.78)	−0.106 (3.28)	−0.001 (0.01)	.68	.39	0.98
5.075 (16.72)	−0.001 (1.84)	0.310 (7.73)					.78	.60	0.91
5.874 (11.08)	−0.001 (0.85)	0.262 (5.17)		−0.001 (0.06)	−0.048 (1.70)	−0.038 (0.34)	.80	.60	0.95

Grade School; Ages 18–65; Original Data

Constant								
5.442	0.000	0.299	−0.009	−0.055	0.069	.68	.40	2.26
(8.99)	(0.002)	(4.57)	(0.71)	(1.70)	(0.62)			

High School; Ages 22–65; Three-year Moving Average

7.469	−0.0004	0.140				.51	.22	1.07
(297.7)	(0.60)	(3.47)						
7.775	0.001	0.081	−0.018	−0.041	0.067	.62	.30	1.24
(29.43)	(1.11)	(1.81)	(2.19)	(1.80)	(1.25)			

High School; Ages 22–65; Original Data

6.217	−0.001	0.165				.67	.43	1.14
(26.52)	(1.30)	(5.57)						
6.647	0.0003	0.129	−0.012	−0.024	0.045	.71	.43	1.25
(17.37)	(0.31)	(3.61)	(1.52)	(1.14)	(0.92)			
5.987	−0.001	0.181	−0.002	0.014	0.003	.44	.09	2.15
(11.34)	(0.35)	(2.88)	(0.19)	(1.01)	(0.04)			

College; Ages 22–65; Three-year Moving Average

7.396	0.006	−0.072				.46	.15	0.65
(64.55)	(2.66)	(0.61)						
8.752	0.008	−0.172	−0.011	−0.134	0.262	.81	.58	1.20
(25.55)	(4.46)	(1.98)	(0.67)	(3.42)	(3.18)			

College; Ages 22–65; Original Data

5.352	0.003	0.249				.60	.31	0.98
(3.98)	(1.27)	(2.62)						
7.692	0.006	0.052	−0.013	−0.126	0.188	.78	.52	1.43
(8.37)	(2.55)	(0.51)	(0.76)	(2.84)	(1.91)			
7.175	0.002	0.073	−0.008	−0.050	0.064	.31	−.14	2.46
(3.99)	(0.39)	(0.36)	(0.28)	(0.68)	(0.27)			

SOURCE: See Table 3.1.

115

TABLE 3.7
COMPARISON OF THE COEFFICIENT OF MALE HOURLY EARNINGS ESTIMATED
DIRECTLY AND ESTIMATED INDIRECTLY FROM ANNUAL EARNINGS

| | | Education Level | | |
	All	Grade School	High School	College
Whites				
Direct estimate	.448	.345	.236	−.068
Indirect estimate	.736	.669	.445	.276
Nonwhites				
Direct estimate	.098	.131	.081	−.172
Indirect estimate	.156	.355	.148	.055

than hourly earnings as an independent variable. A simple trans-formation [30] of the coefficient of annual earnings provides an esti-mate of the coefficient of hourly earnings that is biased by errors of measurement only to zero rather than −1.

Table 3.7 contains direct estimates of the coefficients of hourly earnings alongside the indirect estimates obtained from annual earnings. The indirect estimates are more than 50 per cent larger than the direct ones for all whites and nonwhites and for those with an elementary or high school education. The effect is even more dra-matic for college persons: negative direct estimates are replaced by the predicted positive estimates when annual earnings are used. Even in the large Census sample, the bias toward a negative coefficient resulting from dividing earnings by a badly measured estimate of hours of work may be very large.

Certain systematic variations in hours worked may, however,

---

30. If $\log N_t = b_1 \log E_t + \Sigma b_j X_j$, where E_t is annual earnings at age t; then by subtracting $b_1 \log N_t$ from both sides,

$$\log N_t(1 - b_1) = b_1 \log \frac{E_t}{N_t} + \Sigma b_j X_j,$$

or

$$\log N_t = b_1' \log \frac{E_t}{N_t} + \Sigma b_j' X_j,$$

where E_t/N_t is hourly earnings, and $b_1' = b_1/(1 - b_1)$.

bias the indirect estimates upward. Assume that the true relation is given by [31]

$$\log N = a + b \log w + cz, \tag{3.5}$$

where z represents certain omitted variables that affect N, and where $\log w$ and z are uncorrelated. If w were measured without error, the least squares regression of $\log N$ on $\log w$ would given an unbiased estimate of b. Suppose instead that equation (3.5) is transformed into

$$\log N = \frac{a}{1+b} + \frac{b}{1+b} \log Nw + \frac{cz}{1+b} = a' + b' \log E + c'z, \tag{3.6}$$

where E is earnings. Then $\log E$ and z would be correlated because $\log N$ and z are, and the regression of $\log N$ on $\log E$ would give an upwardly [32] biased estimate of b', and thus of b. If errors of measurement in hours worked were large relative to the error from omitting relevant independent variables, the upward bias in the earnings regressions would be small compared to the downward bias in the hours regressions; and vice versa, if the random error were small compared to the systematic error. In any case, the estimates from regressions of the wage rate and earnings would bound the true value of the wage rate coefficient.

A still different way to reduce the error in measuring wage rates is to utilize recent work on investment in post-school training. If the wage rate is assumed to be proportional to the stock of human capital, and the latter is assumed to be a concave function of work experience when years of schooling are held constant,[33] the wage rate will be a concave function of work experience (e), say the quadratic function

$$w_t = c_1 e + c_2 e^2. \tag{3.7}$$

In a regression of hours of work on this function, c_1 would be positive and c_2 would be negative.

Calendar age is used to measure experience in the results reported in Table 3.8 (post-school age, which Mincer uses, would

---

31. I am indebted for this formulation to James Smith.
32. The bias would be upward as long as $c \neq 0$.
33. Mincer, *Schooling*, gets excellent results with these assumptions.

TABLE 3.8

COMPARISON OF REGRESSIONS CONTAINING AGE AS A MEASURE OF INVESTMENT OF MEN IN POST-SCHOOL TRAINING

(based on three-year moving averages of underlying data)

Dependent Variable [a] (in logs)	Inter-cept	Age	Log Annual Earnings	Log Hourly Earnings	Log Other Income	Log Other Family Income	Log Family Size	Age²	Mult. Corr. Coeff.	Adj. R²	Durbin-Watson
				Independent Variables (t values in parentheses)							
I. Whites											
				All Education Levels							
HW/YR	7.303 (9.53)	0.023 (3.24)	0.129 (1.53)		-0.020 (1.82)	-0.098 (3.92)	-0.241 (6.14)	-0.0003 (3.88)	.98	.96	0.81
5,096 − HW/YR	7.427 (106.7)	-0.026 (8.99)		0.107 (2.04)	0.011 (1.48)	0.100 (10.52)	0.124 (4.75)	0.0003 (9.90)	.98	.96	1.07
				Grade School							
HW/YR	5.820 (6.20)	0.009 (1.25)	0.261 (2.77)		0.001 (0.04)	-0.044 (1.31)	-0.163 (2.59)	-0.0001 (1.68)	.94	.87	0.88
5,096 − HW/YR	7.572 (51.92)	-0.021 (4.39)		0.130 (2.37)	0.006 (0.60)	0.082 (5.81)	0.115 (3.72)	0.0002 (7.34)	.94	.87	0.78
				High School							
HW/YR	6.429 (11.48)	0.010 (2.36)	0.177 (2.92)		-0.025 (2.36)	-0.028 (1.74)	-0.090 (2.59)	-0.0001 (2.83)	.98	.94	0.60
5,096 − HW/YR	7.741 (103.5)	-0.014 (5.47)		0.001 (0.03)	0.021 (2.70)	0.046 (4.62)	0.059 (2.25)	0.0002 (5.395)	.97	.94	0.82

College

HW/YR	6.574 (8.75)	0.022 (1.59)	0.130 (1.38)		−0.058 (3.35)	−0.008 (0.34)	−0.067 (0.63)	−0.0003 (1.96)	.82	.83	0.75
5,096 − HW/YR	8.038 (74.85)	−0.032 (3.88)		0.124 (1.94)	0.045 (3.98)	0.035 (2.21)	−0.018 (0.24)	0.0003 (0.414)	.93	.84	0.73

II. Nonwhites

All Education Levels

HW/YR	6.423 (11.91)	0.000 (0.01)	0.142 (2.48)		−0.002 (0.35)	−0.034 (1.51)	0.134 (2.01)	0.000 (0.15)	.83	.64	1.23
5,096 − HW/YR	7.988 (65.37)	−0.006 (1.96)		0.002 (0.04)	0.004 (1.23)	0.031 (2.35)	−0.026 (0.61)	0.0001 (1.76)	.80	.57	1.24

Grade School

HW/YR	5.164 (7.33)	−0.013 (1.64)	0.370 (4.23)		−0.003 (0.28)	−0.076 (2.26)	0.134 (0.85)	0.0002 (1.50)	.81	.61	0.98
5,096 − HW/YR	7.935 (52.29)	−0.011 (2.60)		0.068 (1.21)	−0.006 (1.03)	0.021 (1.13)	0.134 (1.62)	0.0001 (2.57)	.73	.46	1.02

High School

HW/YR	0.794 (14.11)	0.003 (0.55)	0.109 (2.05)		−0.012 (1.53)	−0.026 (1.21)	0.031 (0.56)	−0.000 (0.51)	.71	.42	1.27
5,096 − HW/YR	7.945 (68.43)	−0.008 (2.13)		0.008 (0.23)	0.011 (2.17)	0.031 (2.27)	−0.005 (0.13)	0.0001 (1.97)	.65	.33	1.27

College

HW/YR	7.784 (8.52)	0.045 (1.37)	−0.036 (0.29)		−0.007 (0.41)	−0.123 (2.79)	0.063 (0.44)	−0.001 (1.20)	.79	.53	1.46
5,096 − HW/YR	8.298 (29.04)	−0.042 (2.87)		0.162 (3.11)	−0.0004 (0.04)	0.064 (2.96)	−0.003 (0.04)	0.001 (2.57)	.85	.65	1.39

SOURCE: Same as Table 3.1.
a. See Table 3.1, note a.

have been better). Usually, age has a positive and age squared a negative coefficient, as predicted by the theory of post-school investment. Moreover, the introduction of age squared into the regression generally lowers the coefficient of earnings, although it remains positive; not surprisingly, the introduction of a second measure of the wage rate decreases the importance attached to the first. The signs of other coefficients are generally not changed.

3.4   WEEKS WORKED VERSUS HOURS WORKED PER WEEK

To separate the response to changes in wage rates of hours per week from the response of weeks per year, regressions similar to those in Tables 3.1, 3.3, 3.5, and 3.6 were run, using as dependent variables hours worked in the census week, consumption hours in that week, weeks worked in 1959, and weeks of consumption in 1959. The results for weeks and hours worked are shown in Tables 3.9 and 3.10.

In the regressions using weeks worked, the coefficient of the male wage rate always has the predicted sign and is generally fairly sizable, although it is typically lower than the corresponding coefficient in the regressions using annual hours. In the regressions using hours worked in the census week, however, this coefficient is not stable, and often has the "wrong" sign and low t values. Apparently, weeks worked respond more systematically than hours worked per week to life cycle changes in the wage rate.[34] The evidence may be spurious, however, because the estimates of hours worked per week have considerably more measurement error than the estimates of weeks worked. As I have repeatedly pointed out, this kind of measurement error biased the regression coefficient for the male wage rate in the direction opposite to my prediction.

3.5   FIRST DIFFERENCES

To reduce the amount of serial correlation in the residuals and to check on the robustness of the findings, regressions like those

---

34. One important exception is the regressions for all male whites, where hours respond more than weeks.

reported in Tables 3.1–3.10 were run using differences between successive ages in the observations on wage rates, hours, other income, family size, etc. Some results with differences in the log of annual hours worked as the dependent variable are reported in Tables 3.11 and 3.12.[35] As expected, the Durbin-Watson statistic is much higher, indicating that the serial correlation in the residuals has been reduced; the correlation coefficient, on the other hand, is much lower, indicating that as usual levels can be explained more adequately than differences.

Otherwise, the first-difference regressions strongly support the level ones: the signs and relative magnitudes of different coefficients are about the same. In particular, the coefficient of the difference in annual earnings is positive, sizable, and statistically significant for both whites and nonwhites in all regressions except those for college persons. This coefficient is somewhat lower for whites and somewhat higher for nonwhites than in the level regressions. Clearly, the first-difference regressions also imply that a rise in the own wage rate over the life cycle induces a reallocation of time toward work and away from consumption.

APPENDIX

1   THE SUBSAMPLES

The 1/1,000 sample from the 1960 Census provides information on over 180,000 individuals.[36] My analysis is confined, however, only to nonagriculture employed men at work during the census week in 1960 who also had been working for earnings in 1959. This sample contains about 34,000 individuals of whom about 31,000 are white and 3,000 are nonwhite.

The sample is divided into eight subsamples, as shown in Table 3A.1. The data in each subsample are grouped by single years of age; the average value of a particular variable at each age is used as the basic observation. The table also contains information about the number of individuals in each subsample, the mean size of the cells, and the coefficients of variation.

---

35. Similar results are found with differences in the log of consumption time as the dependent variable.

36. For a detailed description of this sample, see U.S. Bureau of the Census, *Censuses of Population and Housing: 1960, 1/1,000 and 1/10,000: Two National Samples of the United States* (1969).

TABLE 3.9
REGRESSIONS FOR WEEKS WORKED AND HOURS WORKED PER WEEK OF WHITE MEN
(based on three-year moving averages of underlying data)

Dependent Variable (in logs)	Inter-cept	Age	Log Hourly Earnings	Log Other Income	Log Other Family Income	Log Family Size	Mult. Corr. Coeff.	Adj. R^2	Durbin-Watson
				All Education Levels; Ages 22–65					
HW/WK	3.660 (332.9)	−0.002 (13.75)	0.210 (14.78)				.92	.85	0.49
HW/WK	3.797 (41.22)	−0.002 (2.30)	0.207 (3.29)	−0.007 (0.58)	−0.012 (1.23)	−0.011 (0.25)	.93	.84	0.48
WK/YR	3.731 (375.0)	−0.001 (5.62)	0.175 (13.63)				.92	.84	0.34
				Grade School; Ages 18–65					
HW/WK	3.667 (183.9)	−0.001 (4.24)	0.170 (5.30)				.62	.36	0.65
HW/WK	4.030 (17.61)	−0.001 (1.06)	0.119 (1.99)	0.005 (0.32)	−0.043 (1.99)	−0.026 (0.66)	.72	.47	0.72
WK/YR	3.602 (163.9)	−0.0004 (1.27)	0.321 (9.08)				.86	.73	0.67

Independent Variables (*t* values in parentheses)

High School; Ages 22–65

HW/WK	3.807 (310.8)	−0.001 (5.00)	0.034 (1.79)				.73	.51	0.57
HW/WK	3.729 (42.65)	0.002 (1.57)	−0.117 (1.95)	−0.010 (0.90)	0.003 (0.30)	0.100 (3.69)	.83	.65	1.05
WK/YR	3.650 (189.2)	−0.002 (5.78)	0.326 (10.54)				.88	.77	0.47

College; Ages 26–65

HW/WK	3.730 (173.3)	−0.003 (5.39)	0.154 (5.46)				.68	.43	0.59
HW/WK	3.522 (35.77)	0.005 (3.09)	−0.137 (1.96)	−0.013 (1.26)	0.007 (0.57)	0.238 (4.78)	.85	.69	0.62
WK/YR	3.782 (219.5)	−0.002 (5.53)	0.148 (8.08)				.82	.65	0.49

HW/WK = hours worked per week.
WK/YR = weeks worked per year.
SOURCE: See Table 3.1.

TABLE 3.10

REGRESSIONS FOR WEEKS WORKED AND HOURS WORKED PER WEEK OF NONWHITE MEN

(based on three-year moving averages of underlying data)

Dependent Variable (in logs)	Intercept	Independent Variables (*t* values in parentheses)					Mult. Corr. Coeff.	Adj. R^2	Durbin-Watson
		Age	Log Hourly Earnings	Log Other Income	Log Other Family Income	Log Family Size			
All Education Levels; Ages 22–65									
HW/WK	3.707 (321.4)	−0.001 (6.66)	0.052 (2.73)				.72	.50	1.07
HW/WK	3.834 (36.07)	−0.0004 (1.61)	0.001 (0.03)	−0.010 (3.34)	−0.021 (1.79)	0.052 (2.40)	.84	.67	1.34
WK/YR	3.710 (250.1)	0.001 (3.93)	0.141 (5.82)				.79	.60	0.77
Grade School; Ages 18–65									
HW/WK	3.699 (243.4)	−0.001 (1.62)	0.018 (0.51)				.25	.02	1.00
HW/WK	4.070 (25.26)	−0.001 (0.84)	−0.037 (0.98)	0.004 (0.65)	−0.046 (2.87)	−0.020 (0.30)	.50	.16	1.14
WK/YR	3.682 (196.8)	0.001 (0.91)	0.240 (5.53)				.77	.57	0.71

High School; Ages 22–65

HW/WK	3.779	−0.001	−0.080				.55	.27	1.01
	(224.0)	(1.14)	(2.93)						
HW/WK	3.896	0.0001	−0.104	−0.010	−0.012	0.009	.60	.27	1.10
	(28.02)	(0.17)	(3.31)	(1.73)	(0.74)	(0.24)			
WK/YR	3.690	0.0001	0.220				.81	.64	0.80
	(201.86)	(0.73)	(7.46)						

College; Ages 26–65

HW/WK	3.789	0.001	−0.101				.33	.04	1.15
	(68.45)	(0.81)	(1.77)						
HW/WK	3.947	0.001	−0.140	−0.021	−0.033	0.153	.76	.50	1.62
	(24.79)	(1.64)	(3.16)	(2.66)	(1.66)	(3.72)			
WK/YR	3.607	0.005	0.029				.58	.29	0.56
	(47.71)	(3.45)	(0.37)						

HW/WK = hours of work per week.
WK/YR = weeks worked per year.
SOURCE: See Table 3.1.

TABLE 3.11

REGRESSIONS FOR ANNUAL HOURS WORKED OF WHITE MEN:
FIRST-DIFFERENCE EQUATIONS
(dependent variable: year-to-year differences
in the log of annual hours worked)

Intercept	Δ Log Annual Earnings	Δ Log Hourly Earnings	Δ Log Other Own Inc.	Δ Log Other Fam. Inc.	Δ Log Fam. Size	Mult. Corr. Coeff.	Adj. R^2	Durbin-Watson
	Independent Variables (t values in parentheses)							

All Education Levels; Ages 22–65; Three-year Moving Average

Intercept	Δ Log Annual Earnings	Δ Log Hourly Earnings	Δ Log Other Own Inc.	Δ Log Other Fam. Inc.	Δ Log Fam. Size	Mult. Corr. Coeff.	Adj. R^2	Durbin-Watson
−0.002 (1.82)	0.301 (8.10)					.78	.61	1.60
−0.003 (1.64)	0.351 (5.89)		−0.032 (2.78)	−0.017 (0.67)	−0.103 (1.45)	.83	.66	1.84
−0.002 (0.82)		0.282 (4.14)				.54	.28	1.27
0.000 (0.20)		0.167 (1.56)	−0.026 (1.59)	−0.075 (2.45)	0.039 (0.40)	.66	.38	1.34

All Education Levels; Ages 22–65; Original Data

Intercept	Δ Log Annual Earnings	Δ Log Hourly Earnings	Δ Log Other Own Inc.	Δ Log Other Fam. Inc.	Δ Log Fam. Size	Mult. Corr. Coeff.	Adj. R^2	Durbin-Watson
0.001 (0.41)	0.121 (1.76)		−0.010 (0.92)	−0.014 (0.55)	0.016 (0.17)	.36	.04	2.41

Grade School; Ages 18–65; Three-year Moving Average

Intercept	Δ Log Annual Earnings	Δ Log Hourly Earnings	Δ Log Other Own Inc.	Δ Log Other Fam. Inc.	Δ Log Fam. Size	Mult. Corr. Coeff.	Adj. R^2	Durbin-Watson
−0.0009 (0.35)	0.288 (4.32)					.54	.28	2.07
−0.0003 (0.11)	0.243 (2.99)		−0.022 (1.23)	−0.035 (0.82)	−0.043 (0.36)	.56	.26	2.08
0.003 (0.44)		0.094 (0.07)				.01	−.02	1.10
0.004 (1.02)		−0.108 (1.14)	−0.042 (2.28)	−0.121 (2.82)	0.003 (0.03)	.45	.13	1.21

Grade School; Ages 18–65; Original Data

Intercept	Δ Log Annual Earnings	Δ Log Hourly Earnings	Δ Log Other Own Inc.	Δ Log Other Fam. Inc.	Δ Log Fam. Size	Mult. Corr. Coeff.	Adj. R^2	Durbin-Watson
0.004 (0.61)	−0.065 (0.78)		0.004 (0.28)	−0.028 (0.75)	0.113 (0.89)	.17	−.06	2.91

High School; Ages 22–65; Three-year Moving Average

Intercept	Δ Log Annual Earnings	Δ Log Hourly Earnings	Δ Log Other Own Inc.	Δ Log Other Fam. Inc.	Δ Log Fam. Size	Mult. Corr. Coeff.	Adj. R^2	Durbin-Watson
−0.003 (2.53)	0.290 (8.72)					.81	.64	1.60
−0.002 (1.39)	0.261 (6.45)		−0.026 (3.03)	−0.028 (1.93)	−0.056 (1.47)	.86	.72	2.03
−0.002 (1.40)		0.293 (4.82)				.60	.35	1.41
−0.0002 (0.11)		0.215 (3.23)	−0.035 (3.20)	−0.054 (3.19)	−0.031 (0.62)	.77	.54	2.04

TABLE 3.11 (*continued*)

	Independent Variables (*t* values in parentheses)							
Inter-cept	Δ Log Annual Earnings	Δ Log Hourly Earnings	Δ Log Other Own Inc.	Δ Log Other Fam. Inc.	Δ Log Fam. Size	Mult. Corr. Coeff.	Adj. R^2	Durbin-Watson
High School; Ages 22–65; Original Data								
−0.001	0.154		−0.016	−0.030	−0.066	.54	.22	2.70
(0.20)	(2.90)		(1.76)	(1.76)	(1.12)			
College; Ages 22–65; Three-year Moving Average								
−0.0004	0.161					.49	.21	1.13
(0.14)	(3.38)							
0.003	0.073		−0.025	−0.008	0.162	.59	.27	1.15
(0.93)	(0.86)		(1.76)	(0.36)	(1.48)			
0.003		0.065				.17	.004	0.76
(0.86)		(1.07)						
0.008		−0.160	−0.025	−0.043	0.330	.64	.34	1.18
(2.99)		(2.08)	(1.84)	(2.16)	(3.67)			
College; Ages 22–65; Original Data								
0.004	0.055		−0.015	0.002	0.008	.31	−.01	1.86
(0.87)	(0.94)		(1.40)	(0.11)	(0.07)			

SOURCE: See Table 3.1.

TABLE 3.12
REGRESSIONS FOR ANNUAL HOURS WORKED OF NONWHITE MEN:
FIRST-DIFFERENCE EQUATIONS
(dependent variable: year-to-year differences
in the log of annual hours worked)

	Independent Variables (t values in parentheses)							
Inter-cept	Δ Log Annual Earnings	Δ Log Hourly Earnings	Δ Log Other Own Inc.	Δ Log Other Fam. Inc.	Δ Log Fam. Size	Mult. Corr. Coeff.	Adj. R^2	Durbin-Watson
All Education Levels; Ages 22–65; Three-year Moving Average								
−0.001 (0.21)	0.165 (2.36)					.35	.10	2.12
0.001 (0.44)	0.179 (2.49)		−0.009 (1.18)	0.008 (0.22)	0.157 (1.95)	.49	.16	1.99
0.001 (0.41)		−0.070 (0.90)				.14	.004	1.83
0.003 (0.78)		−0.057 (0.69)	−0.014 (1.79)	−0.004 (0.12)	0.093 (1.04)	.35	.03	1.82
All Education Levels; Ages 22–65; Original Data								
0.002 (0.25)	0.261 (2.71)		−0.022 (2.47)	0.021 (0.44)	0.212 (2.45)	.59	.28	2.72
Grade School; Ages 18–65; Three-year Moving Average								
−0.001 (0.10)	0.350 (3.90)					.50	.24	1.74
0.0003 (0.04)	0.378 (4.26)		−0.022 (1.88)	−0.076 (1.91)	0.012 (0.10)	.59	.29	1.90
0.007 (1.02)		−0.172 (1.50)				.22	.03	1.11
0.006 (0.82)		−0.133 (1.07)	−0.009 (0.63)	−0.056 (1.16)	−0.051 (0.34)	.30	.003	1.20
Grade School; Ages 18–65; Original Data								
0.003 (0.19)	0.366 (4.02)		−0.025 (1.94)	−0.087 (2.27)	0.130 (1.28)	.60	.29	2.81
High School; Ages 22–65; Three-year Moving Average								
−0.001 (0.16)	0.161 (2.77)					.40	.14	2.05
0.0004 (0.09)	0.171 (2.73)		−0.009 (1.19)	0.015 (0.63)	0.046 (0.63)	.45	.12	2.12
0.003 (0.50)		−0.004 (0.06)				.01	−.02	1.78
0.003 (0.61)		−0.009 (0.12)	−0.012 (1.38)	−0.003 (0.12)	0.012 (0.15)	.22	−.05	1.86

TABLE 3.12 (*continued*)

Inter-cept	Δ Log Annual Earnings	Δ Log Hourly Earnings	Δ Log Other Own Inc.	ΔLog Other Fam. Inc.	Δ Log Fam. Size	Mult. Corr. Coeff.	Adj. R^2	Durbin-Watson
				Independent Variables (*t* values in parentheses)				
High School; Ages 22–65; Original Data								
−0.0003	0.148		0.004	0.022	0.012	.26	−.03	2.91
(0.02)	(1.28)		(0.40)	(1.36)	(0.11)			
College; Ages 26–65; Three-year Moving Average								
0.006	0.055					.10	−.02	1.86
(0.48)	(0.61)							
0.005	0.056		−0.014	0.000	0.026	.21	−.07	1.93
(0.39)	(0.59)		(1.06)	(0.03)	(0.18)			
0.012		−0.200				.40	.14	1.84
(0.99)		(2.60)						
0.011		−0.205	−0.010	0.000	0.101	.44	.09	1.87
(0.92)		(2.53)	(0.79)	(0.20)	(0.78)			
College; Ages 26–65; Original Data								
0.003	0.015		−0.017	0.000	−0.188	.21	−.08	2.92
(0.08)	(0.09)		(0.92)	(0.12)	(0.91)			

SOURCE: See Table 3.1.

TABLE 3A.1
SAMPLE SIZE, MEAN SIZE OF CELL, AND COEFFICIENT OF VARIATION IN EACH SUBSAMPLE

Name of Subsample	Years of Schooling	Age Group	Color	No. of Persons	Mean Cell Size	Coeff. of Var.
All-W	All	22–65	white	30,703	698	27
G.S.-W	0–8	18–65	white	8,879	185	39
H.S.-W	9–12	22–65	white	14,726	335	40
Col-W	13+	26–65	white	6,595	165	44
All-NW	All	22–65	nonwhite	2,888	66	35
G.S.-NW	0–8	18–65	nonwhite	1,593	33	36
H.S.-NW	9–12	22–65	nonwhite	1,091	25	61
Col-NW	13+	26–63 [a]	nonwhite	254	7	73

SOURCE: See text note 36.
a. Ages 64 and 65 omitted because of "empty cells."

2   THE VARIABLES

Seven variables are directly available from the 1/1,000 sample, and a number of additional variables were generated by arithmetic manipulation of the averaged ones. The seven directly available are:

		1/1,000 Sample No.
1.	*FS*: Family size (number of persons in the family).	50
2.	*TFI*: Total family income in 1959.	60
3.	*OI*: Total own income in 1959.	43
4.	*RI*: Other own income in 1959.	42
5.	*AE*: Annual earnings in 1959.	39
6.	*HW/WK*: Hours worked during last week before the 1960 Census.	29
7.	*WK/YR*: Weeks worked in 1959.	36

The generated variables are:

8. *HE*: Hourly earnings = $AE/[(HW/WK) \times (WK/YR)]$.
9. *OFI*: Other family income = $(TFI) - [(RI) + (AE)]$.
10. *HW/YR*: Hours worked per year = $(HW/WK) \times (WK/YR)$.
11. *HC/YR*: Hours consumed (not at work) per year = $8,736 - (HW/YR)$.
12. $(HC/YR) - K$: Hours consumed other than on personal care = $8,736 - 3,640 - (HW/YR) = 5,096 - (HW/YR)$.
13. *HC/WK*: Hours consumed per week = $168 - (HW/WK)$.
14. $(HC/WK) - K$: Hours consumed per week other than on personal care = $168 - 70 - (HW/YR) = 98 - (HW/WK)$.
15. *WC/YR*: Weeks consumed per year = $52 - (WK/YR)$.

The unweighted means and standard deviation across different ages of the basic variables used are presented in Table 3A.2.

3   REGRESSION ANALYSIS: REGRESSION FORMS

The logs of the time variables numbered 6, 7, 10, 11, 12, 13, 14, and 15 are used as dependent variables; the logs of the income variables (2, 4, 5, 8, and 9), the log of family size (1), and age are used, in various combinations, as independent variables. The four basic forms used are:

Level regressions
1. Original data
2. Three-year moving averages
First differences
3. Original data
4. Three-year moving averages

All regressions are weighted by the square root of the cell sizes.

TABLE 3A.2

MEANS AND STANDARD DEVIATIONS OF EIGHT VARIABLES
BY EDUCATION-COLOR CLASS; ORIGINAL DATA

	Whites				Nonwhites			
Variable	All-W	G.S.-W	H.S.-W	Col-W	All-NW	G.S.-NW	H.S.-NW	Col-NW
1. Cell size:	698	185	335	165	65	33	25	6.7
	(185)	(71)	(133)	(72)	(23)	(12)	(15)	(4.9)
2. Family size	3.53	3.79	3.51	3.41	3.92	4.37	3.68	3.30
	(0.65)	(0.73)	(0.67)	(0.69)	(0.64)	(0.99)	(0.91)	(1.08)
3. Total family	8,232	6,303	8,105	11,806	5,027	4,328	5,617	6,908
income	(833)	(705)	(910)	(2,124)	(443)	(544)	(1,132)	(2,285)
4. Total own	6,271	4,420	6,126	9,821	3,427	2,825	3,920	4,861
income	(953)	(893)	(889)	(1,951)	(423)	(583)	(945)	(1,764)
5. Other own	282	140	250	684	164	91	381	115
income	(152)	(86)	(184)	(473)	(258)	(93)	(1,117)	(163)
6. Hourly	2.87	2.18	2.77	4.22	1.78	1.54	1.93	2.43
earnings	(0.38)	(0.34)	(0.37)	(0.86)	(0.20)	(0.27)	(0.42)	(0.86)
7. Hours worked	2,102	1,949	2,139	2,221	1,833	1,769	1,890	1,963
per year	(92)	(156)	(68)	(99)	(96)	(183)	(226)	(329)
8. Hours worked	43.6	42.3	44.2	45.0	39.9	39.5	40.9	41.8
per week	(1.1)	(1.7)	(1.0)	(1.6)	(1.5)	(2.5)	(4.0)	(5.0)

NOTE: Means are unweighted; standard deviations are in parentheses. Education-color classes are identified in section 1 of this appendix. Variables are more fully described in section 2.

4   REGRESSION ANALYSIS: PROBLEMS IN ESTIMATION

Empty cells. This problem does not exist in the regressions estimated in the "level original" form, since all regressions are weighted; it does exist, however, in the three other forms, where linear processes (moving averages and first differences) are used. Fortunately, only two cells are empty: ages 57 and 65 among nonwhites with a college education (*Col.-NW*).

The entry for age 57 was estimated as a simple average of the entries for ages 56 and 58, and a cell size of 1 was assigned to this estimate. The same procedure could not be used for age 65 because ages 66 and 67 are also empty. Instead, this cell and the one for age 64 were simply eliminated.[37]

Negative figures. Negative entries create a problem for logarithmic transformations. Negative entries are found only for the variable *OFI* (other

---

37. Age 64 was eliminated because a three-year moving average could not be constructed for that age.

family income). Fortunately, there are only three of these entries, and they all are based on very few observations.[38]

There are several equally arbitrary ways of handling negative values in a logarithmic transformation. Here, I used the original negative value as its logarithmic value. Since the negative entries exceed 100 in absolute value, this method transforms the actual values to positive values close to zero.[39] Fortunately, any bias in this arbitrary procedure is small because the regressions are weighted, and the three cells with negative entries have small weights (each does not exceed 0.4 per cent of the relevant subsample).

---

38. The negative entry for 65-year-old nonwhites with a high-school education is based on only four persons; the negative entries for 60- and 61-year-old nonwhites with a college education are each based on only one person.

39. To use x_0 instead of log x_0 is equivalent to replacing x_0 by e^{x_0} in the original data. If $x_0 < -10$, then $e^{x_0} < 0.00005 \sim 0$.

4

Synthesis and Further Applications of the Empirical Analysis

In Chapter 2, Ghez applied the theory developed in Chapter 1 to cross-sectional data on family consumption of market goods at different ages. In Chapter 3, Becker applied it to cross-sectional data on hours worked by men of different ages. In this chapter, we first use the results for consumption and male time to estimate various parameters of the theory, such as the elasticities of substitution in production and consumption. We then use these estimates to predict the effects on the allocation of goods and time of seasonal, cyclical, and especially secular changes in wage rates. This chapter is more speculative than was the case of the previous two, and we attempt only to suggest how our approach could be applied to time series and other types of data. Therefore, no attention is paid to significance levels, confidence intervals, or other measures of uncertainty of the different estimates and predictions we present here.

4.1 PARAMETER ESTIMATES

The implication of the theory in Chapter 1 is that the elasticity of response of a family's consumption of goods to a change in the

---

NOTE: We are equally responsible for this chapter.

husband's wage rate is given by

$$b_1 = s_1(\sigma_f - \sigma_c) \gtreqless 0 \text{ as } \sigma_f \gtreqless \sigma_c, \tag{4.1}$$

where

$\sigma_f =$ elasticity of substitution in production between any two inputs at a particular time;

$\sigma_c =$ elasticity of substitution in consumption between commodities in different time periods;

$s_1 =$ share of husband's time in cost of producing commodities.

Similarly, the elasticity of response of the husband's time in the non-market sector to a change in his wage rate is

$$a_1 = -[(1 - s_1)\sigma_f + s_1\sigma_c] \leq 0, \tag{4.2}$$

with

$$\sigma_f, \sigma_c \geq 0. \qquad\qquad 0 \leq s_1 \leq 1 \tag{4.3}$$

Equations (4.1) and (4.2) provide only two equations to determine the three parameters σ_f, σ_c, s_1; hence, even if a_1 and b_1 were reliably estimated, not enough information would be available to determine all three. However, a_1 and b_1 are sufficient to determine σ_f, for clearly

$$\sigma_f = b_1 - a_1. \tag{4.4}$$

The relation between σ_c and s_1 is found by substituting equation (4.4) into either equation (4.1) or (4.2):

$$\sigma_c = (b_1 - a_1) - b_1\frac{1}{s_1} = b_1\left(1 - \frac{1}{s_1}\right) - a_1. \tag{4.5}$$

Equations (4.3)–(4.5) place several important restrictions on the values of s_1 and σ_c.[1]

---

1. From equation (4.5),

$$\sigma_c \gtreqless -a_1 \text{ as } b_1 \lesseqgtr 0$$

since $s_1 \leq 1$. By subtracting equation (4.5) from equation (4.4), we obtain $|\sigma_f - \sigma_c| \geq b_1$. Finally,

$$\frac{b_1}{b_1 - a_1} \leq s_1 \leq 1, \tag{i}$$

since $\sigma_c \geq 0$.

The theory in Chapter 1 predicts that an increase in age has the same effect on the consumption of goods and of time (one qualification is developed below). In cross-sectional data of the kind considered in chapters 2 and 3, a unit increase in age changes goods and time by the following amount, if nonmarket efficiency does not change with age:

$$a_4 = b_4 = r'\sigma_c - [s_3 + (1 - s_3)\sigma_c]g_w, \tag{4.6}$$

where

$r' =$ difference between rate of interest and time preference for present;

$s_3 -$ share of goods in cost of producing commodities;

$g_w =$ expected rate of growth over time in real wage rate at given age.

Equation (4.6) helps place useful limits on $r'\sigma_c$, the effect of age on consumption within a given cohort.[2]

As discussed in Chapter 3, a_1 and a_4 are estimated from data in the 1/1,000 sample of the 1960 census. This sample provides information on hours worked, earnings, age, family size, and other income of men. Their consumption time in 1959 is assumed to equal the total time in a year net of estimated time spent on sleep and other personal care minus time spent at work.

The values of a_1, the own wage coefficient, and a_4, the age coefficient, that result from the regression of consumption time of white men on their wage rate, age, and several other variables are reproduced in columns 1 and 2 of Table 4.1; the complete results are given in Table 3.1. The coefficient a_1 is -0.28 for all classes combined, -0.17 for grade and for high school persons, and $+0.05$ for

---

2. If the share of total costs due to wife's time approximately equals the share due to goods, $s_3 \cong (1/2)(1 - s_1)$. Then by substitution of equation (4.5) into equation (4.6), we get

$$r'\sigma_c = a_4 + \frac{1}{2}\left[1 - a_1 + s_1(b_1 - a_1 - 1)\frac{-b_1}{s_1}\right]g_w.$$

By substitution of equation (i), from note 1, above, we obtain,

$$a_4 + \frac{1}{2}\frac{-a_1}{b_1 - a_1}g_w \leqslant r'\sigma_c \leqslant a_4 + (-a_1)g_w, \tag{i}$$

if $\sigma_c(= b_1 - a_1) \geqslant 1/2$. The inequality signs are reversed if $\sigma_c < 1/2$, and these limits are identical if $\sigma_c = 1/2$.

TABLE 4.1
Regression Coefficients from Time and Goods Regressions:
1/1,000 and BLS Samples

Group	Effect of Male Wage Rate on Male Time (a_1) (1)	Effect of Age on Male Time (a_4) (2)	Effect of Earnings on Goods (b_1) (3)	Effect of Age on Goods (b_4) (4)
All persons	−.28	.002	.55	.002
Grade school	−.17	−.001	.51	.003
High school	−.17	−.001	.48	.005
College	.05	−.004	.61	.003

Source: Tables 3.1 and 2.4.

college persons; a_4 is +0.002 for all classes combined and negative for each of the three education classes (see the discussion in Chapter 3 for the effects of measurement and systematic error on these estimates).

A completely independent source, the Bureau of Labor Statistics Survey of Consumer Expenditures for 1960–61, provides information on family consumption classified by age of the head, family size, family income, and family earnings; the latter are not broken down to show wage rates and hours worked of different family members separately. The results of a regression of family consumption on the head's age, family size, property income, and family earnings used as a proxy for the head's wage rate are presented in Chapter 2. The coefficients of earnings, b_1, and of age, b_4, are reproduced in columns 3 and 4 of Table 4.1: b_1 ranges from +0.48 for high school persons to +0.61 for college persons, and b_4 ranges from +0.002 to +0.005.[3]

---

3. Since the BLS Survey does not report wage rates but annual earnings, which are affected by the substitution toward market time induced by a rise in wage rates, Ghez also developed a regression of family consumption on wage rates, age, and other variables from the 1/1,000 Census sample. The estimates of b_1 range only from +0.46 to +0.52 for the three education classes, or slightly below those using earnings and other BLS data (the estimate of b_1 for all classes combined is, however, +1.04 with the Census and only +0.55 with the BLS data). Similarly, the estimates of b_4 range from +0.001 to +0.009, somewhat larger than the range using BLS data (again, however,

Using equation (4.4) and the estimates of a_1 and b_1 in columns 1 and 3 of Table 4.1, we derived the estimates of σ_f, the elasticity of substitution in production, shown in column 1 of Table 4.2. The elasticity equals $+0.83$ for all education classes combined, and ranges from $+0.56$ to $+0.68$ for the individual classes. The upper bounds on σ_c, the elasticity of substitution in consumption, shown in column 2 of Table 4.2, are derived by using equation (4.6), the estimates of a_1, and the fact that $b_1 > 0$. These upper bounds are always small, never exceeding 0.28. Lower bounds on the difference between σ_f and σ_c are shown in column 3: substitution is apparently much easier in production than in consumption since the difference is never less than about one-half.

A comparison of columns 2 and 4 of Table 4.1 shows that a_4 and b_4 are the same for all education classes combined, whereas b_4 is different in sign and several tenths of a percentage point larger for the separate classes. Much of the difference is due to the secular decline in family size, a variable not included in equation (4.6). An increase in family size significantly increases the consumption of goods (see, for example, Table 2.2), and slightly reduces the time allocated to the nonmarket sector by men (see Table 3.1 and the discussion in that chapter). Therefore, a secular decline in family size would reduce the consumption of goods and increase the consumption time of men in younger cohorts relative to older ones. That is, in cross-cohort data typified by the Census or BLS surveys, a secular decline in family size would increase the effect of age on consumption (b_4) and reduce its effect on men's time (a_4). Since the elasticity of goods with respect to family size averages about $+0.25$, and that of male time about -0.02, the 0.72 per cent annual decline in birth rates since 1909 would result in an increase of 0.0018 in b_4 and a decrease of 0.00014 in a_4. The algebraic difference between these effects, $+0.002$, is more than a third of the observed difference between b_4 and a_4.

This explanation suggests that a_4 is a better estimate of the variables included in equation (4.6) than b_4 because a_4 is hardly affected by changes in family size. Then, by using equation (i) from note 1

the estimates for all classes combined are quite different: -0.003 and $+0.002$). Since, apparently, the biases in estimating b_1 and b_4 by using earnings rather than wage rates are not very great, we rely in this chapter on the estimates obtained by using the BLS data.

TABLE 4.2

ESTIMATES OF PARAMETERS OF MODEL

Group	Elasticity of Substitution in Production ($\sigma_f = b_1 - a_1$) (1)	Upper Bound on Elasticity of Substitution in Consumption ($\sigma_c \leq -a_1$) (2)	Lower Bound on Difference Between σ_f and σ_c ($\sigma_f - \sigma_c \geq b_1$) (3)	Bounds on Effect of Age on Consumption Within Cohort[a] (4)	Lower Bound on Share of Husband's Time in Cost of Producing Commodities $\left(s_1 \geq \dfrac{b_1}{b_1 - a_1}\right)$ (5)
All	.83	.28	.55	.007 ≤ .010	0.66
Grade school	.68	.17	.51	.003 ≤ .004	0.75
High school	.65	.17	.48	.003 ≤ .004	0.74
College	.56	−.05	.61	−.007 ≤ .007	1.09

SOURCE: Table 4.1. Symbols are defined in Table 4.1 and in accompanying text.

a. Bounds are determined by equation (i) in note 2 of text.

above, and the estimates of a_4, we can derive the bounds on $r'\sigma_c$, the effect of age on consumption within a given cohort, shown in column 4 of Table 4.2.[4] The range is quite small within each education class but differs considerably from class to class: the midpoint declines from $+0.0085$ for all persons to $+0.0035$ for both elementary and high school persons to negative values for college persons. The size of all the midpoints except the last one suggests a significant positive effect of interest and time preference combined on consumption. If r', the difference between interest rates and time preference, is taken to be $+0.10$, the size of the midpoint for all persons implies that $\sigma_c = 0.085$; if $r' = +0.05$, $\sigma_c = 0.17$.

How do these estimates compare with those obtained in other ways? The elasticity of substitution in production can be estimated directly by combining the BLS and Census samples to get ratios of factor quantities and factor prices. The ratio of factor quantities equals family consumption of goods and services (from the BLS) divided by the consumption time of men (from the Census); the ratio of factor prices equals the wage rate of men (Census) divided by unity, the numeraire price of goods and services. In a regression of the log of the ratio of quantities on the log of the ratio of prices, the resulting regression coefficient is a direct estimate of the elasticity of substitution in production.

Table 4.3 contains the results when family size, age, other male income, and earnings of other family members are also included as independent variables in the preceding regression. These direct estimates of the elasticity of substitution are very similar for each of the education classes; they average about $+0.47$, and are about 0.15 less than the indirect estimates reported in column 1 of Table 4.2. The direct estimate for all classes combined, on the other hand, is about 0.25 larger than the indirect estimate.[5] These regressions, like those run separately for goods and time, indicate that an increase in family size or age, especially the former, increases the consumption of goods relative to male time.

---

4. The value of g_w is set equal to 0.0274, the actual rate of growth in real wages in the United States between 1909 and 1967. See U.S. Bureau of the Census, *Long Term Economic Growth, 1860–1965* (1966) and various BLS reports for the figures from 1964–67.

5. Both the direct and the indirect estimates are biased by systematic and random errors in hours worked. It is not clear which set of estimates contains the larger bias.

TABLE 4.3

DIRECT ESTIMATES OF ELASTICITY OF SUBSTITUTION IN PRODUCTION

Education Class [a]	Inter-cept	Independent Variables (t values in parentheses)					R^2	Adj. R^2	Durbin-Watson
		Log Wage Rate	Log Male Nonwage Income	Log Other Family Income	Log Family Size	Age			
All	−0.308	1.09	−0.06	0.28	0.60	−0.002	.90	.78	1.37
		(3.16)	(−1.01)	(3.31)	(2.34)	(−0.297)			
Grade school	−2.45	0.48	−0.05	0.18	0.74	0.007	.74	.48	1.63
		(1.83)	(−1.04)	(1.59)	(3.19)	(1.29)			
High school	−2.18	0.50	−0.06	0.15	0.75	0.010	.86	.71	1.34
		(1.46)	(−1.31)	(1.90)	(4.28)	(1.65)			
College	−2.50	0.42	0.09	0.11	0.96	0.006	.93	.85	1.27
		(1.72)	(1.88)	(1.45)	(4.75)	(1.072)			

SOURCE: Gilbert R. Ghez, "A Theory of Life Cycle Consumption" (Ph.D. diss., Columbia University, 1970).
a. Age range of head of household is 22 to 65.

The low estimates of the elasticity of substitution in consumption between different time periods are consistent with the dominant opinion of professional economists, which is based on a belief that consumption is not very responsive to changes in interest rates. If the elasticity of substitution in consumption were small, the rate of growth over time in consumption would not be very responsive to limited changes in the rate of interest since

$$d\,\frac{d \log C}{dt} = d\,\frac{d \log X}{dt} = d\,\frac{d \log L}{dt} = \sigma_c dr, \tag{4.7}$$

where C, X, and L are the consumption of commodities, goods, and time, respectively, and dr is the change in the rate of interest. If σ_c were about $+0.10$, a change in the interest rate by two percentage points would change the rate of growth in consumption by only two-tenths of one percentage point. If, however, the difference between the interest rate and time preference were reduced to zero, the rate of growth in consumption also would be significantly reduced, by more than four-fifths of a percentage point according to the mid-point estimate of $r'\sigma_c$ for all education classes combined.

Estimated lower bounds on s_1, the share of husband's time in the cost of producing commodities implied by the values of a_1 and b_1 in Table 4.1, are presented in column 5 of Table 4.2. These bounds are all extremely high, the lowest being 0.66. An upper bound on s_1 can be obtained if property income and the value of wife's time are assumed to be negligible, and if s_1 is equated to the ratio of the time spent by men in the nonmarket sector exclusive of personal care to the total time of men exclusive of personal care. This ratio is about 0.60 for all men in the Census sample (see notes 24 and 25 in Chapter 3), less even than the lowest bound in Table 4.2. The estimates of s_1 derived from the estimates of a_1 and b_1 are, therefore, implausibly high, which again indicates that $-a_1$ is underestimated (relative to b_1). The upward bias in s_1 implies a downward bias in s_3, and thus, by equation (i) in note 1, above, a downward bias in the estimated effects of age on consumption within a given cohort.

4.2   SEASONAL, CYCLICAL, AND SECULAR CHANGES

Although both the theoretical and empirical analysis in Chapters 1, 2, and 3 focuses exclusively on life cycle variations, it has important implications for the effects of seasonal, cyclical, or secular changes in wage rates and other parameters. We first consider seasonal changes, which offer the most promising test of our approach. It is a reasonable assumption that knowledge of the presence of a persistent seasonal in wage rates is usually widespread. Our theory predicts that if $\sigma_f > \sigma_c$, then the consumption of goods and hours worked would both increase during the seasons when wage rates are relatively high. If our empirical estimates of these elasticities also hold for seasonal changes, they imply, in particular, that a 25 per cent seasonal increase in wage rates would increase the consumption of goods by about 12 per cent and hours worked by perhaps 10 per cent.

Casual evidence strongly indicates that employment responds positively to a seasonal in wage rates, but little is known about the seasonal response of consumption. A significant seasonal response of total consumption would be difficult to explain by errors in predicting the future, changes in permanent income, capital market rationing, or other variables used in consumption functions, and would provide a powerful confirmation of our theory.

The well-known procyclical responses of aggregate consumption and employment can also be explained by our theory, but they can be plausibly explained too by errors in forecasting cyclical fluctuations in incomes, capital market rationing, and other considerations. More persuasive evidence of a substitution of goods for time when wage rates are cyclically high, and time for goods when they are cyclically low, can be found in a study by Grossman of the effects of unemployment on the relative consumption of different goods.[6] He argues that male unemployment should cause a relatively large reduction in expenditures that are close substitutes in household production for male time, whereas female unemployment should cause a relatively large reduction in expenditures that are close substitutes for female time. In Table 4.4, we compare the reductions in expenditures on different goods when heads of families (mainly men) are unemployed with the reductions when other family members (mainly women) are unemployed. Unemployment of the latter reduces expenditures on household operations and personal care by a large amount relative to the effects on these categories of unemployment

6. See Michael Grossman, "Unemployment and Consumption: A Note," *American Economic Review* (March 1973).

of the head, presumably because a woman's own time is the best substitute for these expenditures. The same is true for clothing, but to a smaller extent. Substitution of time for goods in household production would result in a procyclical fluctuation in goods and market time even if "permanent" income and interest rates did not fluctuate cyclically.

Still another important application is to secular trends in consumption and "leisure" (i.e., nonmarket uses of time). Although both trends have been studied extensively, they have not been related to each other. Columns 1 and 2 of Table 4.5 contain annual rates of growth in real consumer expenditures and in nonmarket time between 1909 and 1967, and for various subperiods. Both time and goods have grown significantly over the whole period and in the different subperiods, but goods always have grown much faster. The difference between these rates of growth, shown in column 3, indicates that the annual rate of growth of goods has exceeded that of time by about 1.6 percentage points for the period as a whole.

TABLE 4.4

PERCENTAGE REDUCTIONS IN EXPENDITURES ON VARIOUS
CONSUMPTION ITEMS AS A RESULT OF UNEMPLOYMENT
RELATIVE TO CHANGE IN ALL EXPENDITURES

Item	Head Unemployed	Member Other than Head Unemployed
Food	0.7	0.7
Housing and utilities	0.8	0.4
Household operations	1.0	4.2
House furnishings	1.0	0.6
Clothing	1.6	2.5
Medical care	1.4	0.5
Transportation	1.1	0.9
Personal care	0	1.4
Tobacco and alcohol	1.0	0.9
Reading and recreation	0.9	1.3
Other	1.4	0
Saving	30.4	33.1

SOURCE: Michael Grossman, "Unemployment and Consumption: A Note," *American Economic Review* (March 1973).

TABLE 4.5
ANNUAL RATES OF GROWTH IN REAL CONSUMER EXPENDITURES,
NONMARKET TIME NET OF PERSONAL CARE, AND REAL WAGE RATE,
1909–67

Period	Real Consumer Expenditures per Capita ("Goods") (1)	Nonmarket Time (2)	Difference Between Goods and Time (3)	Real Wage Rate (4)	Predicted Difference Between Goods and Time (real wage rate × σ_f)	
					$\sigma_f = .8$ (5)	$\sigma_f = .65$ (6)
1909–67	1.99	.40	1.59	2.74	2.19	1.78
1909–29	2.14	.33	1.81	2.47	1.98	1.61
1930–48	1.62	.65	0.97	3.44	2.85	2.34
1949–67	2.18	.23	1.95	2.60	2.08	1.69
1930–67	1.89	.45	1.45	3.03	2.48	1.89

$\sigma_f =$ elasticity of substitution between goods and time.

SOURCE: Col. 1 from U.S. Bureau of the Census, *Long Term Economic Growth, 1860–1965* (1966). Col. 2: 1909–58 from Edward Denison, *The Sources of Economic Growth in the United States and the Alternatives Before Us* (New York: Committee for Economic Development, 1962); 1958–67 from U.S. Dept. of Labor, *Manpower Report of the President* (various dates, 1958–67). Col. 4: 1909–63 from Census, *Long Term Economic Growth;* 1964–67 from various BLS reports.

According to a simple version of our theory, a secular rise in real full wealth *alone* would cause both goods and time to rise at the same rate; therefore, if real wage rates also grew secularly, goods would rise faster than time because goods would be substituted for time in the production of commodities. The predicted difference between the rates of growth in goods and time would equal the rate of growth in real wage rates (column 4 of Table 4.5) multiplied by the elasticity of substitution in production (σ_f).

We take 0.8 as the estimated elasticity (σ_f) for all white men and 0.65 for men with elementary or high school education (see Table 4.2, column 1), and multiply each by the rate of growth in wage rates. We can then derive the predicted differences between the rates of growth

TABLE 4.6
Predicted Rates of Growth in Goods and Male Time, 1909–67

Period	Predicted Growth in Goods		Predicted Growth in Male Time	
	$\sigma_f = .8$ (1)	$\sigma_f = .65$ (2)	$\sigma_f = .8$ (3)	$\sigma_f = .65$ (4)
1909–67	2.41	2.16	.22	.38
1909–29	2.17	1.95	.20	.35
1930–48	3.03	2.72	.28	.48
1949–67	2.34	2.05	.21	.36
1930–67	2.76	2.48	.25	.44

$\sigma_f =$ elasticity of substitution between goods and time.

in goods and male time shown in columns 5 and 6 of Table 4.5.[7] The predicted differences always exceed the actual ones (in column 3) when the elasticity is assumed equal to 0.8: by small amounts during the periods 1909–29 and 1949–67, and by large amounts during 1909–67 and 1930–48. When the elasticity is assumed equal to 0.65, the predicted differences are close to the actual ones except during 1930–48.[8]

If time series observations on goods and nonmarket time can be interpreted as the successful working out of "lifetime" plans, and if all wealth elasticities equal unity, the rate of growth in goods will equal the sum of the rate of growth in real wealth and the substitution in production toward goods induced by the growth in real wage rates.[9] Similarly, the rate of growth in nonmarket male time will equal the difference between the rate of growth in real wealth and the net substitution away from male time induced by the growth in real wage rates.

---

7. For these predictions, we assume that male and female wage rates grow at the same rate, and that the elasticity of substitution between aggregate goods and male time equals that between aggregate goods and female time.

8. The predicted differences are overstated because the secular decline in family size, which lowers the rate of growth of goods relative to male time, is ignored.

9. We ignore any secular change in the productivity of household production.

Rates of growth in goods predicted from the rates of growth in real wealth and wage rates are shown in Table 4.6, columns 1 and 2. Real wealth is assumed to grow at a rate equal to the difference between the rates of growth in money wage rates and a weighted average of goods prices and these money wage rates, the weights being the share of each in household production.[10] Since we have not been successful in estimating these shares, the share of time is arbitrarily set equal to 0.60 and that of goods to 0.40. The substitution effect toward goods equals the product of the share of time, the rate of growth in "real" wage rates, and the elasticity of substitution in production between goods and time.[11] For column 1, we assume an elasticity of substitution of 0.8, whereas for column 2, we assume 0.65 (these are the estimates reported in Table 4.2). Actual and predicted rates of growth are rather close for the periods 1909–29, 1949–67, and 1909–67, especially when 0.65 is used, but the predictions are far above the actual values for the depression-war period 1930–48.

Predicted rates of growth in nonmarket male time equal the difference between rates of growth in real wealth and the substitution in production away from male time induced by the growth in male wage rates; the latter equals the product of the share of goods, the rate of growth in wage rates, and the elasticity of substitution in production between goods and male time. Again, the predictions based on an elasticity of substitution equal to 0.65, given in column 4 of Table 4.6, are usually closer to the actual values: very close for 1909–67, 1909–29, and 1930–67 as a whole, but much too low in 1930–48 and too high in 1949–67.

The secular trends in goods and male nonmarket time are, therefore, reasonably well explained even by a simple version of our theory. These trends have not been integrated by the traditional analysis because the substitution between time and goods in the production of commodities induced by the secular rise in wage rates has been ignored.

---

10. That is, $\bar{W} = \bar{w} - (s_g \bar{p}_g + s_t \bar{w})$. But since

$$\bar{w} - (s_g \bar{p}_g + s_t \bar{w}) = \bar{w} - \bar{p}_g - [(s_g - 1)\bar{p}_g + s_t \bar{w}]$$
$$= \bar{w} - \bar{p}_g - (s_t \bar{w} - s_t \bar{p}_g)$$
$$= \bar{w} - \bar{p}_g - [s_t(\bar{w} - \bar{p}_g)] = s_g(\bar{w} - \bar{p}_g),$$

therefore,

$$\bar{W} = s_g(\bar{w} - \bar{p}_g).$$

11. The assumptions made in note 8 also apply to these estimates.

Index